Celebrate

Catering ideas for perfectly imperfect home gatherings

Introduction

If the pandemic has taught us anything, it would be when the opportunity is available, we should get together to celebrate!

I have always loved planning my children's parties and cooking up a storm whilst creating memories for Christmas and Easter. This book will give you lots of ideas for creating beautiful parties in your home.

I have been cooking in commercial kitchens for 30 years from small restaurants to enormous kitchens on Hayman Island and other large hotel kitchens. I had 7 years as the chef and owner of my own restaurant and have been involved in loads of event management and catering for a multitude of different locations and occasions. I have organised an event for 150 people in a location without a kitchen and delivered a 7-course degustation with wines and canapes. Now as a mum of three children I have a lot of fun planning their birthday parties. I need to make sure I am enjoying the occasion with them and not creating too much work for myself with fancy food!

I really hope that this book will inspire you to have more confidence on planning that special party or event. I hope it will help to make beautiful memories with the people you love, whilst enjoying great quality food. I have put together all my best tips and tricks to pull off a great celebration. Enjoy!

Eloise Emmett 2022

Acknowledgments

Thanks to the generous sponsors as without them, this book would be not be possible. Thanks for their enthusiasm and ease to work with and of course the beautiful products they produce for me to enjoy creating recipes with.

Bream Creek Vineyard

Campo De Flori

Petuna

Rannoch Quail

Tasmanian Lavender Company

Tassal

Tropic Co Prawns

Thank you to my family, my husband Brendan and children Maggie, Stephanie and Oscar who are happy to pop on a good shirt for a photo and enjoy all the foods. Thanks to Maggie for writing all the party game ideas out for me, and to Stepanie for making the Vanilla Cakes and Easter Cake.

Thank you to my sister Blaise for making the awesome Digger Cake.

Thanks to my Mum for proof reading the book when I have looked over everything so many times I just can't see errors!!

Thanks to my Aunty, Kylie from Stokely 9 Design, for the design of this book.

It certainly is a family affair isn't it!

Thanks to my workshop, event and dinner guests at Little Norfolk Bay Events and Chalets, who taste all the recipes and inspire me to create new dishes.

And finally, thank you to you for purchasing this book and supporting my small business. There are only two people involved in the production of this book, the designer Kylie, my bestie from Stokely 9 Design and The Art of Words Studio, and me. Unlike a published book that has a big budget and many staff involved. Although I have edited until my eyes go blurry about 200 times and I am not that great at sitting in front of a computer at the best of times, I am sure there will be the odd mistake or two. Let's hope they are little grammatical typos and not additional cups of chillies or something hideous like that! Please let me know if you see anything so I can fix for future print runs. Email me at eloiseemmett@gmail.com. Hopefully you can see them as little quirks in this handmade product, that is totally produced in Tasmania and printed in Australia!

Recipes, photography and words © Eloise Emmett

Design © Kylie Berry

No part of this book can be copied without permission, includes photocopying and photos of the pages.

Although I have researched the dietary information and other info carefully (for about 30 years!!) it is still only my opinion, so please always talk to a health professional. I will not be liable for any injuries or damage as a result of following the information and recipes in this book.

Planning

I cannot stress enough how important planning is for your event. Organise what you need to do 6 weeks out, one week out, the day before and on the day. A stress-free and fun event requires a lot more than just a shopping list bought the day before then an epic mission on the day of the event.

I always get told how calm I am and how I make it look so easy, but it's because a massive amount of effort has gone into the planning and thinking through the details. And really think through what you can do and what's the purpose of the occasion. If it is your child's birthday, it is about them having a great day with their friends. You don't want to be snapping at the birthday child while you assemble an overcomplicated cake.

Think about what you can realistically get done in the time you have available. So maybe making the lamingtons for a train cake the month before so they can be quickly iced in the morning and topped with lollies for a super easy cake will take the pressure off the day. Or if you are having a small dinner party and decided on paella for a main, which needs you to be standing at the stove while your guests are there, then keep the entree and dessert super simple. Perhaps something pre made to simply pull out of the fridge, like a pickled octopus salad and summer berry pudding. You'll find all the suggestions through this book of when you can make it.

Invitations

Send the invites out 4-6 weeks before the event. Weddings and engagement parties can be sent out around 3 months before. For a wedding send out a save the date especially for those who would be expected to travel to attend the event up to a year before.

There are loads of beautifully designed invitations available to buy commercially but handmade invites are always cute and fun for the kids to make, a really great rainy day activity. I am emphasising low waste in the book, moving away from cheap plastic stuff from the discount stores, purchases we really do not need, where we can. You can design quite fancy invites on iPhone apps these days. A photo with the information printed on it is always an easy choice.

Facebook messages and text messages are a great way to invite people but I still prefer a printed invite that is stuck on the fridge as a reminder.

Put an RSVP date on the invite with a week out from the event. If you have not heard from guests - which can be rude of them - or there may be a reason why. The invite may have got lost, the invite is still in the school bag, they have sent a text to the wrong RSVP number, or they may have a lot going on. Any parent of a few kids will have experienced all these reasons and more, I have been on the giving and receiving end of most of them!

Chase them up with a quick message such as "just checking you received the invite to Oscar's party on the 6th of November. I am finalising the catering so can you please confirm if you are attending or not?". This is especially important if it will impact your catering. Also keep in mind if you get invited and you cannot attend let the host know as soon as you can.

If you have a group of family that are always non-committal and unreliable, then keep that in mind with your planning so you do not get frustrated when you have left over food. Make sure to have plans in place for what to do with it.

Your invitation needs this information:

To

Occasion

Date

Start time (and finish time where applicable)

Dress code (where applicable)

Address

RSVP to and how

Table Settings

While it might seem pretty basic and not worth writing about, back in my day of hospitality training at the old Drysdale Tafe when I was completing a food and beverage service course, we were taught how to set a table. In the real world this procedure has been put in place many times. I have also frustratingly watched many clearly not trained front of house managers spend far more time than necessary setting a dining room. One particular large wedding comes to mind when very well meaning family members were left in charge of setting the tables and I happened to walk past when they were starting setting the cutlery without the chairs at the table. I did interrupt this one for a quick lesson, if they had set the entire tables without the chairs they would of needed to reset it all when the chairs went into place! What a waste of time on an already frantic morning!!

Place tables where you want them. Be mindful of space to walk around and where people are facing, and not too close to toilet doors or kitchen doors where you can. Wipe over tables and chairs. Lay the table cloths on tables. Place chairs in place evenly spaced and slightly pushed in under the table. Lay cutlery on the table, fork in position for left hand and knife for right hand making sure they are lining up with the chairs. First course cutlery on the outside working your way in through courses to the dessert or main cutlery inside. Alternatively the dessert cutlery can sit above the cutlery. Place glasses above knives and the bread plate sits outside of knife.

Everything around 2cm from the edge of the table. Knife blade facing middle, the napkin in center 2cm from edge of table.

Then table decorations on in the space that is available. I love big vases of flowers and foliage and I just pick what I have in my yard but they are really annoying and block people from seeing each other when actually seated at the table, so plan to remove them when everyone sits. Make sure you have somewhere other than the floor, where they will get kicked, to sit them. A few spare tables will do. Laying some flowers and foliage on the actual table when setting the table will look nice when all the vases have been removed.

My version of the perfect Christmas tree, is one filled with hand made craft from my children.

Decorations

As tempting as it is to use the cheap single use plastic decorations from the cheap chain stores, they really are just a waste when they are pulled down and thrown in the bin after their few hours use - contributing to a landfill nightmare. Making some decorations, preferably from something we need to recycle, is loads of fun for children for all occasions and makes them part of the celebration. The kids will love coloring in a bunting for birthdays, Easter or any occasion.

I am sorry but I am very judgy of those parents who put the guard around the Christmas tree so the kids can not touch it and other hideous stories of not displaying the kids craft and having the perfect tree! Where is the fun in that? Our Christmas tree decorated with love on the first of December always looks 'interesting' by Christmas day, when it has had a month in our sunny living area and most of the leaves have been vacuumed off the floor! Oh well, at least it is a source of a lot of laughs on Christmas day when we are hosting (see our 2021 Christmas Tree!!).

Big bunches of flowers or foliage always look great. Go foraging and see what you can find. Beautiful handmade ceramics always look gorgeous too.

Celebrate - Catering ideas for perfectly imperfect home gatherings

Menu Design

Traditionally when we plan a menu we would choose the lighter dish first and then move through to the heaviest. For example, oysters, quail then red meat. However, there are always exceptions, we might serve a venison carpaccio before a fish main. I find it easiest to simply not serve any food a guest may be allergic to. Remember as I have previously suggested what you are capable of doing and why are you hosting the event?

ALLERGIES

A word on allergies. If there is a guest with allergies, intolerances or food preferences it is not your responsibility to cater for them, but if you want to that's great. My kids have friends who are celiac and diabetic so I take this into consideration when planning and if the party is small I just keep everything at the party suitable for them. Also a good excuse for me to keep the sugar/junk consumption low anyway! But it should not be expected that you cater to every dietary preference and you try to cater for every intolerance it is extra expense, and time for you and when a potential life threating allergy may slip through if you are flustered.

If the guest brings it up, you can let them know what you are providing and politely suggest they can BYO which is actually easier for those people and parents as they have the foods on hand. For a children's party, if you always make sure you have a big fruit platter and veggies and veggie dips on the table then that covers most allergies anyway and the parents with the child will know the best GF sausage roll or mini pizza and will probably have packets in their freezer anyway. In my experience they send food along anyway just in case.

With the invites I would suggest not requesting dietary requirements as you may end up catering for a wide range of preferences. I believe dumping your food "choices" on the host is bad manners, if you are invited somewhere you politely accept and if the food is not to your satisfaction/preference then don't eat it, simple.

One of the biggest bonus of cooking from scratch is you know what is in all the food! Obviously if it's a health risk the host needs to know to inform the guest what to avoid, but unfortunately as in the professional setting I have seen 40 out of 100 guests have a food intolerance/allergy/preference, I am not exaggerating. 20 years ago we would see the odd allergy or vegetarian!! This makes it difficult for the kitchen or in the home setting, the host. It also makes it dangerous for people with serious anaphylactic conditions like my daughter Maggie, or if you have a celiac they cannot just pick the flour out it is crucial the flour is not anywhere near their food, and this is what the kitchen staff need to be focusing on. An example I have seen with my own eyes, someone chooses a gluten free lifestlye for their health but occasionally has a slice of pizza. Then I don't think it is reasonable to expect the chef at a wedding they are attending to make sure their jus does not have a pinch of flour in it. If it is not anaphylactic or make them sick, the guest can eat what they like and pick around it.

WASTE

Did you know food waste has an enormous impact on the planet? Eating discretionary foods (food we don't need to survive) is also a waste. However we can all enjoy a few treats at a party whilst being mindful of waste. It is important to include some nutrition, which isn't hard when cooking real food, otherwise it is all just waste! Pickled octopus and spinach pie is delicious so I will choose this to bring along to a party to nibble on, and at least I know I am consuming some greens and protein.

So to limit waste, its great to understand portions sizes.

HOW MUCH TO BUY

When working out what to buy a guide for a meal for an adult is:

- 100-200 grams meat or fish
- 1-2 cups veg
- ½ to 1 cup starch

So if you are having 10 people for dinner and the menu is

- Oysters
- Beef wellington
- Lemon tart

You'll need to buy:

- 2 ½ dozen oysters, 3 oysters per person (60 grams per person)
- 1-1.5 kilo beef (with the oysters thats 160-210 grams protein)
- 1 kilo spuds
- 2 kilo carrots, beans and broccoli

HINTS

Buy fresh where you can like breads and meat so any extra can be frozen if not eaten.

Cook foods that can be frozen if not used, for example for my children's parties I will make some scones and apple tea cakes that take no time to prepare and can be frozen if not eaten and popped in the school lunches the following weeks.

How you serve the food will impact waste, for example sometimes plating up the meal, although a little more effort is a lot less waste than buffet style. Or serving a crayfish cocktail dished up into a gorgeous individual dish, that way everyone gets a taste rather than feeling like you need to provide a lot to go on a buffet style meal.

If it is a cocktail style event 8-12 pieces per person. 6-8 plus a one or 2 mini meals. If its canapes before a meal 3-4 pieces per person.

Celebrate - Catering ideas for perfectly imperfect home gatherings

Kids Birthday Parties

How much do kids love a party to look forward to? The play centers and kids party places do an amazing job and are a great choice. I know when Brendan was working away and the kids were younger a play center with a donut cake with supermarket donuts was all I could manage some years. But it's nice to have something at home as well, especially if you are watching your budget. I hope you find this information helpful as I have planned plenty of kid's parties now. I think at Maggie's first birthday and still in commercial chef mode I had a tonne of food leftover so I now have a much better idea!!

I also think young kids would think a few snags on the BBQ some fairy bread and a jelly is an amazing party so there really is no need to go overboard... that is if you do not want too. There is absolutely nothing wrong with spending weeks constructing tee pee tents if that's what you want to do too!

We have listed some game suggestions in here. If the kids are happy playing and having fun then just leave them, there is no point breaking up their fun to get them to play a game or eat food. Maybe have a few things set up to encourage play? Like a mud kitchen or sandpit. Games are really for ice breakers or for everyone to get to know each other or if you feel a child needs to be included or is being left out. Maybe when you've got a few school friends mixed with some after-school activity friends it can be a great way for people to get to know each other or make everyone feel included. If you have some games prepared and then they are not played it is no big deal. But there is nothing more frustrating than kids that are playing happily to be broken up to sit bored to tears for 20 minutes with one of those long boring politically correct pass the parcels where everyone gets a prize, especially when they are young and their attention spans are limited.

Maggie has kindly written out party game suggestions and instructions at the back of this book.

4 and under

For the very young 1st birthdays or even 2nd or 3rd birthday, the child might not have many friends to invite. At this age toddlers tend to wander around each other rather than play, so the party may be more a family or adult catch up. If so, you might want to look further in the book for ideas.

Try to keep the guest list low. 4 friends makes a nice party at this age but expect some can't make it.

Keep the party about 1.5 – 2 hours long and put an end time on the invite. This may not seem like a long event but trust me it will be the longest one and a half hours of your life supervising half a dozen 2 or 3 year olds!!

If you are having a 10 am morning tea or 2 pm afternoon tea time, keep the food simple. Fruit platter, fruit salad or fruit stick per person, veggie sticks and dip, then and 3-4 pieces per person of more filling items. ie one sausage roll, one party pie, one sandwich, one jelly. Then finished off with the party cake - this is plenty of food.

Having a batch of scones or some simple apple tea cakes made is a good idea in case they eat more than you plan, and if they aren't needed can be popped in the freezer for lunchboxes or another day.

If it's a 12-noon party then you are providing a meal. This will mean you need 6-8 pieces of food per person or one mini burger and 3-4 pieces. If you have invited kids then only cater for the children. If you expect or ask the parents to hang around to supervise then a cheese platter and a dip and a cup of tea is polite, or if they are invited as a family then you will need to cater for each guest.

Games

- Pass the parcel
- Piñata
- Sleeping lions (have a few prizes for this great at the end of a rowdy party!)
- Dancing competition

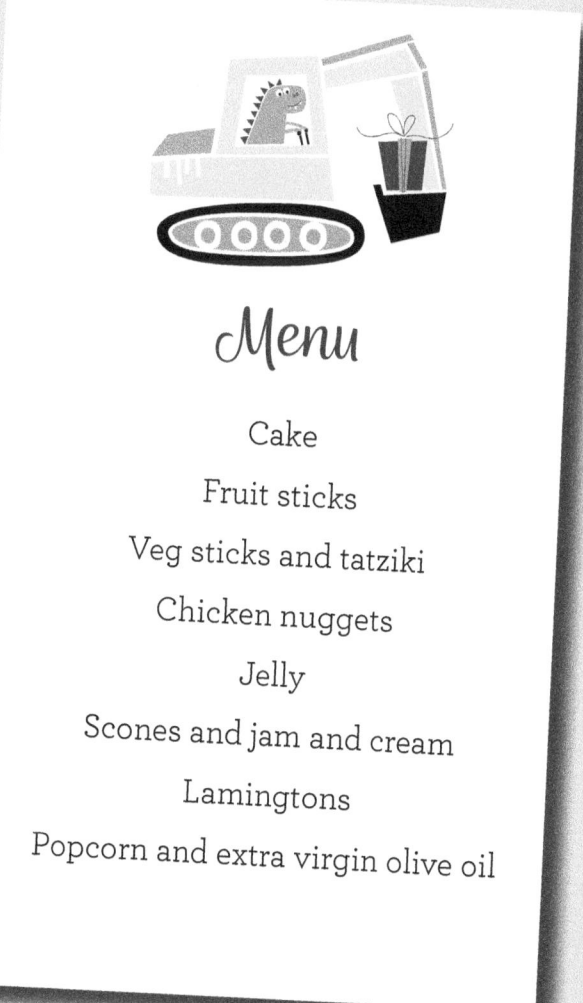

Menu

Cake

Fruit sticks

Veg sticks and tatziki

Chicken nuggets

Jelly

Scones and jam and cream

Lamingtons

Popcorn and extra virgin olive oil

4-8 year olds

Try to keep the guest list low, 6-8 friends makes a nice party at this age but except some can't make it.

Keep the party about 2 hours long and put an end time on the invite.

If you are having a 10 am morning tea or 2 pm afternoon tea time, keep the food simple. Fruit platter, fruit salad or fruit stick per person, veggie sticks and dip, then and 4-6 pieces per person of more filling items. ie one sausage roll, one party pie, one sandwich, one jelly. Then finished off with the party cake - this is plenty of food.

Having a batch of scones or some simple apple tea cakes made is a good idea in case they eat more than you plan, and if they aren't needed can be popped in the freezer for lunchboxes or another day.

If it's a 12-noon party then you are providing a meal. This will mean you need 6-8 pieces of food per person or one mini burger and 3-4 pieces. If you have invited kids then only cater for the children. If you expect or ask the parents to hang around to supervise then a cheese platter and a dip and a cup of tea is polite, or if they are invited as a family then you will need to cater for each guest.

I do not restrict what I let my kids eat at parties but I always lay out fruit and veg to start with and then serve the main course (burger etc.) and then bring out the sweets and the kids chosen party food as I figure they can't fit too much in after nutrient dense lunch.

Games

- Piñata
- Sleeping lions (have a few prizes for this great at the end of a rowdy party
- Dancing competition
- Pass the parcel only a few wraps they lose interest at this age
- Bobs and statues
- Bobbing apples
- Musical Chairs

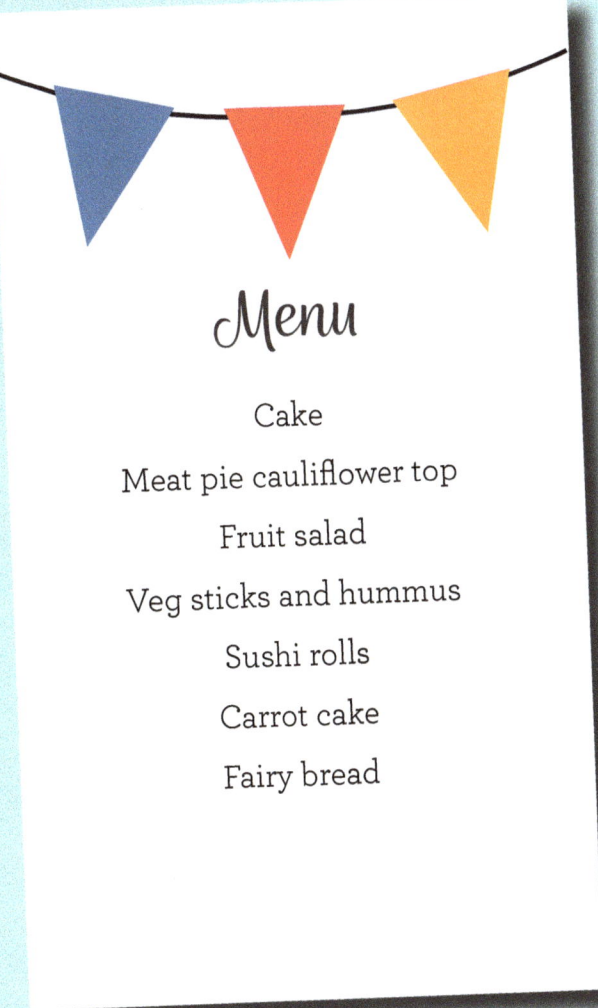

Menu

Cake

Meat pie cauliflower top

Fruit salad

Veg sticks and hummus

Sushi rolls

Carrot cake

Fairy bread

8-12-year olds

Try to keep the guest list low, 6-8 friends makes a nice party at this age but except some can't make it.

Keep the party about 2 hours long and put an end time on the invite.

If you are having a 10 am morning tea or 2 pm afternoon tea time, keep the food simple. Fruit platter, fruit salad or fruit stick per person, veggie sticks and dip, then and 4-6 pieces per person of more filling items. ie one sausage roll, one party pie, one sandwich, one jelly. Then finished off with the party cake - this is plenty of food.

Having a batch of scones or some simple apple tea cakes made is a good idea in case they eat more than you plan, and if they aren't needed can be popped in the freezer for lunchboxes or another day.

If it's a 12-noon party then you are providing a meal. This will mean you need 6-8 pieces of food per person or one mini burger and 3-4 pieces. If you have invited kids then only cater for the children. If you expect or ask the parents to hang around to supervise then a cheese platter and a dip and a cup of tea is polite, or if they are invited as a family then you will need to cater for each guest.

At this age they are ready for sleepovers, discos, high teas or even a crafty activity like a cake decorating party or making pizza, shell mobiles, bracelets or other crafty type activities instead of or with a few party games.

Games

- Musical chairs
- Dancing competition
- The tray game
- Blindfolded makeup challenge
- Treasure hunt

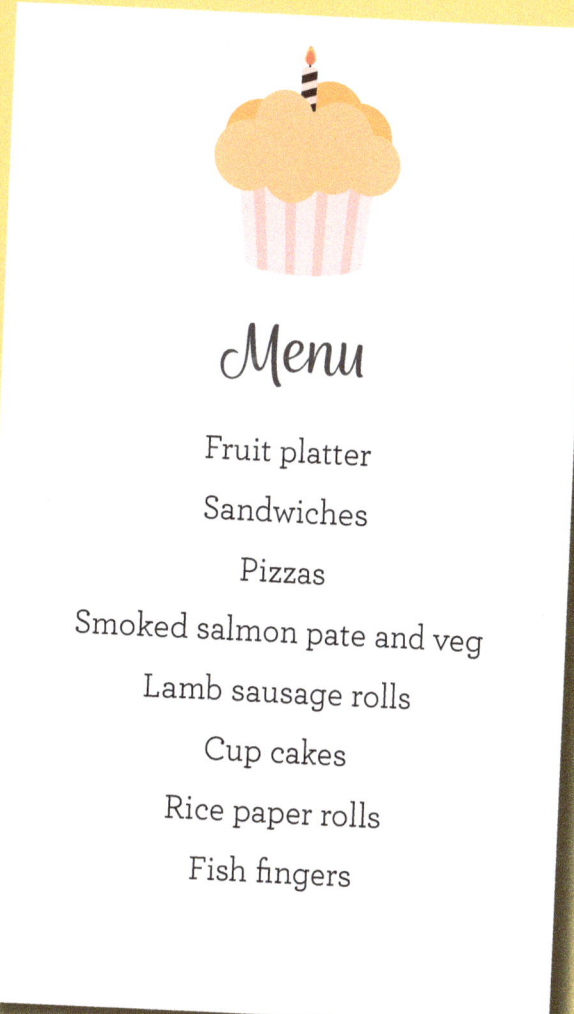

Menu

Fruit platter

Sandwiches

Pizzas

Smoked salmon pate and veg

Lamb sausage rolls

Cup cakes

Rice paper rolls

Fish fingers

13-17 year olds

Growing teenagers are hungry so make sure there is plenty of food for whatever time you are having the party. If its a meal serve a full meal or 10-12 pieces per person canape style, or if it is a morning tea or afternoon tea 6-8 pieces per person. At this age they may want to do a craft activity as part of the party like cake decorating, have a disco or sleepover. I think I will be sticking with daytime parties for my teens in fear of alcohol turning up uninvited to the party.

Party Theme Ideas

- Sleepover- tents
- BBQ
- High tea
- Brunch
- Picnic
- Disco

Games

- Musical chairs
- Dancing comp
- Bobs and statues
- Selfie Hunt
- Donut eating
- Tray game
- Sentence jumble
- Animal freeze

High Tea Menu

Caramel slice

Sandwiches

Quiche

Lamingtons

Scones with jam and cream

Savoury scones

Eclairs

Macadamia pie

Lemon tart

18th and 21st Birthdays

Personally, I'll be trying to organise parties for these ages that are not a big booze fest. I don't think I want the responsibly of young adults mixed with alcohol. I helped my sister organise a gorgeous picnic in a beautiful garden for her 21st and 20 years later she still has people tell her it's one of the best 21st birthdays they have been to.

Party Ideas

- BBQ
- Plated Buffet
- Cocktail party style nibbles with mains
- Brunch
- High Tea

Menu Idea

- Fancy picnic nibbles canapes and mains standing:

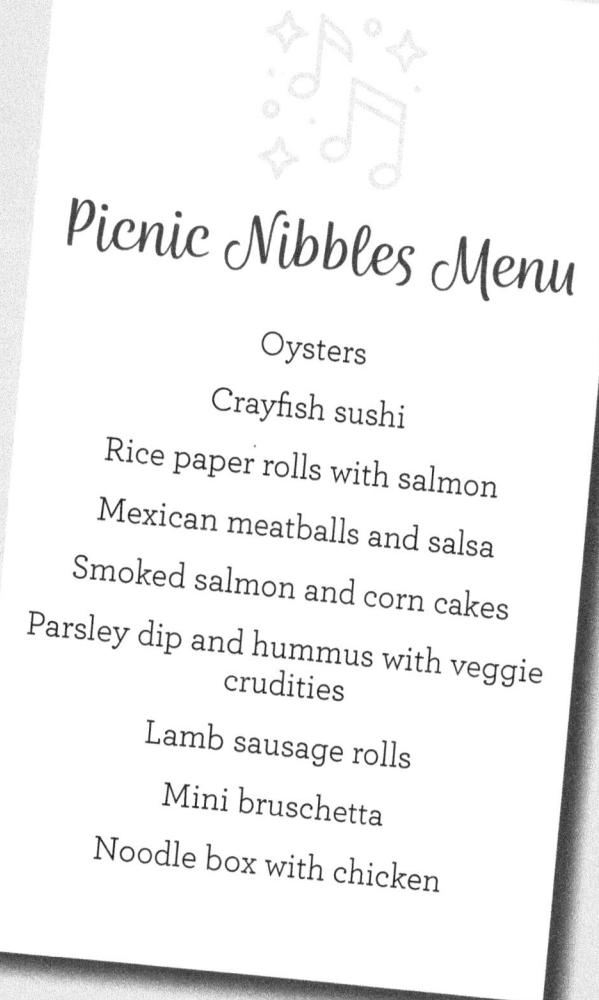

Picnic Nibbles Menu

Oysters

Crayfish sushi

Rice paper rolls with salmon

Mexican meatballs and salsa

Smoked salmon and corn cakes

Parsley dip and hummus with veggie crudities

Lamb sausage rolls

Mini bruschetta

Noodle box with chicken

Christmas

The lead up the Christmas is lots of fun with the kids to make cakes, puddings, gingerbread houses and more. I have included a few recipes for fun things to take to parties in the lead up to Christmas and ideas for your Christmas day feast. Throw my portion size catering recommendations, which I suggest earlier in the book, out the window at Christmas as when you have hosted Christmas it is nice to have loads of leftovers for the next few days!

Ideas for Christmas parties

- Cheese ball tree
- Seafood antipasto wreath (pictured left)
    - Warmed olives
    - Hummus
    - Pickled Octopus
    - Smoked salmon
    - Spinach Pie
    - Crayfish

Christmas Menu

Turducken

Beef wellington

Pea mint salad

Beetroot goats cheese salad

Potato and tomato salad

Christmas pudding and kahlua custard

Easter

Good Friday is always a fun seafood feast and I generally can't resist filling up the deep fryer with extra virgin olive oil and cooking some super fresh fish in beer batter with a few potato cakes. There are plenty of ideas in my book Seafood Everyday and my famous seafood chowder is always popular on many people's Good Friday lunch menu. A traditional roast is always great for Easter Sunday lunch. I have suggested here a menu for a smaller group for Easter Sunday lunch.

Good Friday Menu

Potato cakes and taramasalata

Beer battered fish

Seafood chowder

Oysters

Prawn saganaki

Grilled octopus and haloumi

Salmon glazed with lemon myrtle and honey

Easter Sunday Menu

ENTREE

Quail with honey mustard and apple

MAIN

Paella

DESSERT

Creme brulee

Engagement Party

This can be formal or casual event. A grazing table is always a good looking and delicious catering option, but be mindful of hygiene. I am old school and like a lot of containers on the spread to keep everything separate. I don't like the meats touching the fruits or seafood dribbling on the biscuits and cheese like we see on those Instagram grazing tables where it is all plonked on the table!

Ideas

- BBQ
- Grazing Table
- Cocktail party
- Buffet or plated buffet
- Lunch
- High tea
- Picnic

Grazing Table Menu

Parsley dip
Smoked salmon dip
Cheese
Fruit
Meat
Pickled octopus
Smoked salmon

Wedding

I guess the ultimate event is deciding to cater for your own wedding at home, or at a friends place with a magnificent garden or something unique and special. Some may think your nuts but we did it mainly because we wanted to be married on the Peninsula and at the time there were not many options and we thought we could do it better ourselves. I am all for a good party and celebration but when I hear of people spending a house mortgage deposit on a fancy wedding it really blows my mind. Absolutely fine if you have wealthy parents who are paying the bills but for those who will be paying themselves especially, while working and having a family, education and activity costs to think about, or they may already have children who need the money spent on them for education or other practical expenses or it's the second marriage they realise it's just one day.

Think about who will help. Are there a few responsible young adults on the family fringe that would like some cash? Maybe hiring a private chef or caterer and shipping it out is an option? Or just a chef for the night? It also does not have to be a boozy dinner and evening affair - maybe a high tea in the garden somewhere suits the family's better? There are no rules on what you can do for your wedding.

Themes

- High tea
- Lunch
- Grazing table
- Nibbles cocktail party
- Nibbles with mini meals standing
- Buffet
- Plated buffet
- Fancy or non fancy BBQ
- Spit roast and salads
- Plated up meal

Menu idea

Sit down dinner menu served platted buffet style to the table

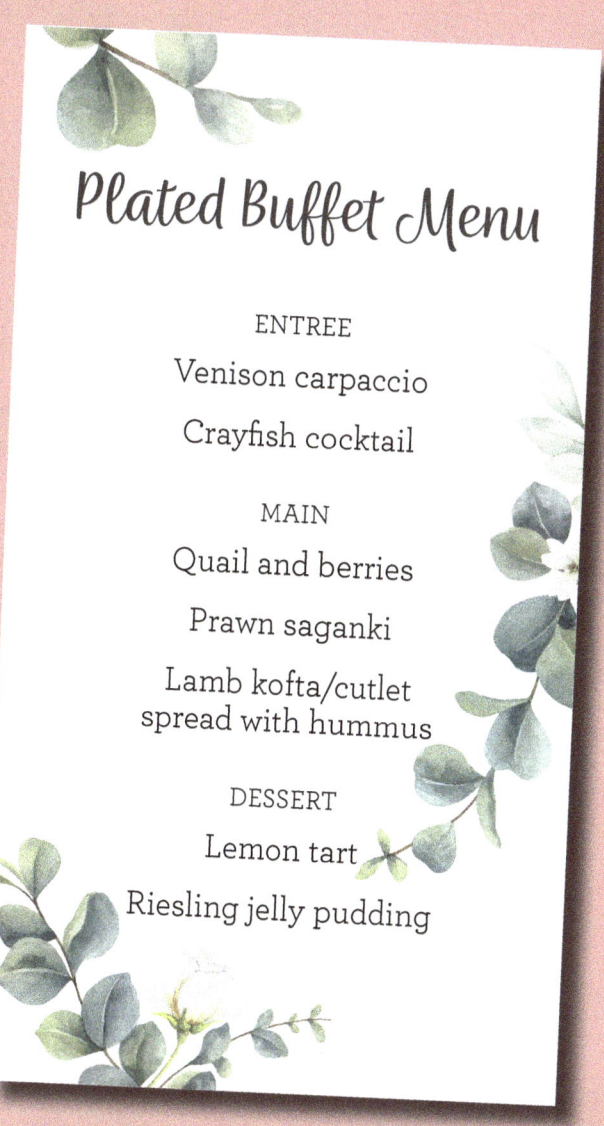

Plated Buffet Menu

ENTREE
Venison carpaccio
Crayfish cocktail

MAIN
Quail and berries
Prawn saganki
Lamb kofta/cutlet spread with hummus

DESSERT
Lemon tart
Riesling jelly pudding

Baby Shower

Generally, some games are played, food is eaten and everyone watches the gift opening. Morning and afternoon tea events are popular for baby showers. Provide 6-8 pieces of food per person for morning or afternoon tea. Or a brunch is a nice option with food that can be prepared and shared at the table. Homemade croissants are the ultimate special occasion breakfast, with some smoked salmon and brie cheese or jams.

Ideas

- Brunch
- Morning tea
- High Tea
- Lunch
- Afternoon tea
- Grazing table

Games

- Guess when the baby is due
- Peg game
- Tray game
- (Please see page 163 for more details)

Brunch Menu

Croissants
Clafutis
Homemade baked beans
Scrambled eggs
Bacon
Mushrooms

BREAM CREEK VINEYARD

Bream Creek Riesling Jelly Strawberry Pudding

SERVES 6-8

A simple and delicious dessert that can be pre-made and easy to serve at the event.

1 bottle Bream Creek Riesling

20 grams gelatine

500 grams strawberries

200 grams lady finger biscuit (or make a sponge cake)

250 grams cream cheese

150 grams cream

1 teaspoon vanilla essence

50 grams sugar

Bring the wine to a simmer in a heavy based pot and dissolve the gelatine, allow to cool slightly and transfer to a serving dish add in chopped strawberries and biscuits. Leave to cool and set.

Whip cream cheese, cream, vanilla and sugar together well and pour on top of set jelly, top with fresh strawberries.

RANNOCH QUAIL

Grilled Rannoch Quail with Berries

SERVES 4 FOR AN ENTREE

Half a large quail is sufficient for an entree and one large quail is enough for a main course. Deboned quail are surprisingly easy to cook on the BBQ or in a pan. When it is berry season I love this combination of a few simple ingredients to create a delicious meal. The hot smoked Rannoch Quail is an excellent product and a good alternative to take the pressure off cooking when needed, for example when it is a large function or other courses require more fuss and attention. So substitute with hot smoked quail to make this even easier to serve.

2-4 Rannoch Quail - boned

extra virgin olive oil for cooking

sea salt

pepper

2 tablespoons balsamic vinegar

2 tablespoons extra virgin olive oil

2 cups berries

2 cups salad leaves

Mix the olive oil and balsamic together well add the berries and leaves just before serving.

To cook the quail on the flat grill of a BBQ or in a pan cook for around 4 minutes on each side over a medium heat until cooked through, season well with sea salt and pepper and serve with the salad.

Caramel Slice

MAKES 16

My favourite!! Absolutely essential for a party!!

BASE

1 cup plain flour

½ cup brown sugar

½ cup desiccated or shredded coconut

125 grams butter

FILLING

800 grams sweetened condensed milk (2 cans)

4 tablespoons golden syrup

120 grams butter

TOPPING

125 grams cooking chocolate

60 grams copha or coconut oil

Preheat the oven to 180°C.

Line a 3cm deep lamington pan.

Combine all base ingredients in a bowl or thermocooker. Mix well. Press into prepared lamington pan. Bake for 15 to 20 minutes, or until light golden. Remove from oven. Cool.

Make filling by mixing all filling ingredients in a heavy based saucepan or thermocooker over medium heat. Cook, stirring, for about 5 minutes or until golden. Pour over cooked base. Bake for 10 minutes or until cooked. Cool completely. Refrigerate for 2 hours or until set.

To make the topping place chocolate and copha into a heat-proof bowl over a saucepan of simmering water. Stir until melted. Pour over caramel. Refrigerate to set. Cut into squares to serve.

Cob Loaf

SERVES PLENTY

This is my mum's party favourite and I have also introduced delicious salmon into it instead of bacon on occasion. I have found fish eating vegetarians love salmon rashers, so yum! Use hot smoked salmon or smoked salmon and try different cheeses. Use more mix and scrape more bread out depending on how many people it is for or use less mix and serve it on the side of a soup for a smaller group for lunch.

1 cob loaf

½ bunch parsley

3 large spring onions

200 grams bacon

100 grams mozzarella cheese

100 grams cream cheese

50 grams parmesan cheese

50 grams sour cream

salt and pepper

Slice the top of the cob loaf and scoop out the bread, leaving around about a strong and solid 1.5 cm walls, put the bread to the side we will heat this up later to dip back into the cheesy goodness.

Finely slice the spring onion and chop the parsley, grate the cheeses and mix with the sour cream and cream cheese and the bacon rashers that are sliced into a 4 mm slice. Season with salt and pepper.

Fill the cob with the cheese mix, put the lid on and wrap in foil and bake in a 160°C oven for about 20 minutes or until the cheese mix is hot and melted in the middle. Wrap the extra bread from the middle in foil and heat for about 5 minutes and serve with the loaf. Serve immediately.

Chicken, Mushroom and Leek Lasagne

SERVES 8

This beautiful lasagne is delicious enough to serve as a main for a dinner party with handmade pasta, but also makes a lovely weeknight meal. It can be prepared the day before the event. When your guests are in your house you don't want to be fusing in the kitchen trying to cook a chicken breast or similar that is easily ruined when overcooked!

1 kilo chicken thighs

1 tablespoon extra virgin olive oil

2 onions

4 cloves garlic

½ large leek white

200 grams mushrooms

800 grams tomato

1 tablespoon basil

1 tablespoon oregano

2 tablespoons tarragon

PASTA

200 grams flour

2 eggs

CHEESE SAUCE

2 tablespoons butter

70 grams plain flour

600ml milk

100 grams cheddar

100 grams fetta

salt and pepper

salad to serve

Preheat the oven to 180°C.

To make the pasta, put the flour into a large bowl and make a well in the middle. Add the eggs to the flour and combine. Turn out on to a clean surface or board and then knead well for at least 5 minutes until the pasta is smooth. Using a pasta machine set at number 1 (or at the widest opening setting) feed the dough through the pasta machine. Repeat this process 3-4 more times increasing the setting to a higher setting each time until the pasta is approximately 2mm thick and silky smooth.

To make the chicken sauce, dice the onion and leek and crush the garlic, then sauté them in a heavy based pan until soft. Add the diced chicken thigh, tomato, mushrooms and herbs. Simmer for 20 minutes.

To make the cheese sauce, melt the butter in a heavy based saucepan and add the flour and stir until combined. Add the milk gradually, stirring continuously until the sauce is thick and smooth. Add the cheeses, stir through and season with salt and pepper. In a lightly greased baking dish or tray, layer the meat and pasta sheets for 3-4 layers and top with the cheese sauce. Bake for 30 minutes until the top is golden brown and the lasagne is cooked through.

Rice Paper Rolls

SERVES 12

Keep them simple for a children's party or spice them up for a delicious canape or entrée with something a bit fancy like prawns or crayfish.

12 rice papers

1 cup thin rice noodles

1 carrot

3 spring onions

½ bunch Vietnamese mint or mint leaves

1 capsicum

1 small cucumber

add fresh chillies or pickled jalapenos

avocado

1 chicken breast
(cray fish, raw fish, raw tuna, prawns)

1 teaspoon extra virgin olive oil

soy sauce to serve

To make the filling, pop the rice noodles in boiling water to soften.

To cook the chicken breast, add the olive oil into a heavy based pan and sauté the chicken on a medium heat for about 7-10 minutes each side or until cooked through. Thinly slice the capsicum and spring onion (lengthways), grate the cucumber and carrots and shred the mint leaves. Once the chicken has cooled, shred the chicken breast with a fork and put in a bowl. Add the other ingredients and combine well.

Making one roll at a time, soak each rice paper in hot water for about 30 seconds until soft and then carefully remove and set aside on a flat clean surface or board. Place the mixed ingredients in the middle of the rice paper, fold in the sides of the rice paper then roll up tightly. Refrigerate to soften, before serving with a light soy sauce.

Pizza and Scrolls

MAKES 2 LARGE PIZZAS OR 12 SMALL PIZZAS OR SCROLLS

The ideas for pizza and scrolls are limitless. You can top with fetta, rosemary and garlic for a fancy dinner party starter or ham and cheese for the kid's party. Other ideas include BBQ chicken, salami and olives and meatlovers. Pizza dough can be made the day before or even in advance and frozen, just make sure it has been brought back to room temperature before shaping and cooking. A nice bread to start can really add to a simple meal.

500 grams flour

1 teaspoon yeast

1 teaspoon sugar

1 teaspoon salt

320 grams warm water

TOMATO BASE

1 onion

2 cloves garlic

1 tablespoon extra virgin olive oil

400 grams tomato

1 tablespoon basil

1 tablespoon oregano

sea salt

cracked pepper

To make the sauce, it can be made in bulk and frozen or a few days before the event for the flavours to develop. Peel and chop the onion and dice and peel and crush the garlic and sauté in a heavy based pot with the oil until translucent. Add the tomato, herbs and salt and pepper and simmer over a low heat for around 30 minutes until cooked.

Preheat the oven to 200°C.

To make the dough knead all ingredients well, I use the thermocooker or you can use any mixer or knead by hand on the bench for around 10 minutes to produce a smooth firm dough.

Cover and leave to rise in a warm position until the dough has doubled in size. Knock the dough back down and divide into 2 and roll into tight balls.

Roll the dough out into 2 large (around 30cm diameter) pizza bases or 20 small pizzas pile with your toppings of choice. Or roll out into a large square and roll up and then cut into wheels to lay on a baking tray to bake as scrolls.

If you like a thin base be ready to cook your pizza straightaway. If you like it thicker leave it to rise after you have put your toppings on.

Bake for around 15-20 minutes or until golden brown and cooked through.

Tropico Co Prawn Saganaki

SERVES 4

We all love a delicious main course that is easy to serve while guests are over. This one can be made before, even the day before and in the fridge ready to pop in the oven. You could use raw prawns simply give them a flash fry in olive oil before laying in the baking dish. Use small individual portion dishes for a cute presentation.

smoked paprika

1 red capsicum

2 onions

5 cloves garlic

2 tablespoons extra virgin olive oil

1 tablespoon basil

1 tablespoon oregano

black pepper

pinch salt

600 grams tomato

1 kilo cooked Tropic Co prawns

lemons

100 grams fetta

green salad to serve

Roast the capsicum drizzled with extra virgin olive oil in a hot oven. Cool and peel. In a large heavy based frying pan sauté the onion and the garlic until translucent.

Add tomatoes, herbs, pepper, salt, paprika and capsicum and simmer for around 20 minutes, lay peeled prawns in a baking serving dish and pour tomato over.

Sprinkle fetta over and bake with a grill setting for 15 minutes until heated through and cheese is melted. Serve with fresh squeezed lemon and a green salad.

Homemade Fish Fingers (or Chicken Nuggets)

MAKES 10

While I understand most people who buy my books and cook may wonder why I include such basic recipes. I still think this is an important recipe to include. Sadly those boxes of nuggets and fish fingers sometime only contain 50 percent fish or chicken EKKK whats in the other 50 percent? And they may be made overseas with who-knows-what quality produce, we know some fish is practically farmed in sewers overseas. It is not hard or time consuming to crumb a few pieces of actual chicken or fish, Oscar does this on his own and he has been for years. Have them done the day before with a few extra crumbs and bake on the day. The home made versions are delicious and I actually enjoy eating them myself with home made chutney or tartare.

500 grams firm white fish or 2 chicken breasts

½ cup flour

1 egg

½ cup milk

1 cup bread crumbs

extra virgin olive oil or olive oil spray

Lay the fish flat on a board and cut into 5 flat discs length ways. Crack the egg into a bowl and beat in the milk. Dip each piece of fish in the flour, shaking off excess flour over the bowl. Dip each piece of fish into the egg mix and then into the breadcrumbs. Heat a little oil in a heavy based pan over a low heat, shake off the excess breadcrumbs and then panfry the nuggets for about 3 minutes on each side until golden and cooked through.

Serve with home-made chutney and a fresh crispy salad.

Spinach Pie

SERVES A LOT

My favourite use of big bunches of silver beet from my garden.

1 onion

1 clove garlic

1 tablespoon

extra virgin olive oil

200 grams spinach or silver beet leaves

150 grams fetta cheese

150 grams ricotta cheese

80 grams parmesan cheese

1 tablespoon basil

1 tablespoon oregano

salt and pepper

50 grams butter

1 packet filo pastry

Preheat the oven to 180°C.

To make the pie, finely chop the onion and garlic. Heat the extra virgin olive oil in a heavy-based saucepan over medium heat and sauté the onion and garlic until softened. Add the spinach and continue to sauté until just cooked. Drain any liquid from the saucepan and set aside to cool.

Grate the parmesan cheese, and crumble the fetta. Stir the ricotta, parmesan and fetta cheeses through the spinach mix and season with salt and pepper. Melt the butter and set aside.

Carefully unwrap the filo pastry and separate into 4 equal portions. Use ¼ of the pastry sheets to line the bottom of a medium-sized baking tray, brushing each sheet with butter before layering with the next. Top with of the spinach mix.

Repeat the layering process in the same manner, ensuring that the top layer is pastry. Brush the top with melted butter and bake for 15-20 minutes or until the pastry is golden brown.

Vanilla Cake and Butter Cream

DOUBLE LAYER 18CM CAKE.

This is a simple and delicious sturdy cake for a layered cake. Layered with jam and buttercream and coated in buttercream it can be decorated with all sorts of chocolates, biscuits, sweets, wafers or flowers. The cake can be made a month in advance and frozen. It would be hard work to muck this super sturdy yet delicious cake up!! Cake decorating credit in this image goes to Stephanie Emmett at her 11th Epic Cake decorating party! Each guest had a double layered cake to decorate and a bench full of icings, sprinkles, colours, biscuits and chocolates. It kept them very entertained for a few hours. When else do you get a chance to decorate a big cake when you are 11?!!

400 grams butter

400 grams caster sugar

8 eggs

pinch salt

4 teaspoon vanilla essence

400 grams self-raising flour

In a large mixing bowl and strong arm or your mixer of choice beat the sugar and butter together until creamy. Beat in eggs one at a time, beat in vanilla and fold through flour. Pour into prepared tins and bake for around 25 minutes or until golden and cooked through.

Butter Cream

2 cups icing sugar

½ cup butter

dash milk

food colouring

Whip room temperature butter and then whip in icing sugar until smooth and creamy add a dash of milk if needed.

Paella

SERVES 8

I love the story of paella but I don't know how true it is. That is was the men turn to cook so they all came together and threw whatever they had in a big pan. The chicken and chorizo add the flavour so never omit them for fancy ingredients, it never works.

1 onion

extra virgin olive oil

3 cloves garlic

400 grams chicken wings

2 chorizo sausage

2 cups spinach

pinch Campo de flori saffron threads

1 cup paella rice

1 teaspoon smoked paprika

1 teaspoon oregano

3 cups chicken stock (approximately)

1 cup peas

3 large ripe tomatoes

400 grams mussels

Soak the saffron threads in a little water, preferably overnight.

Chop the onion and crush the garlic and fry in the oil over a medium heat add the chicken and brown and the chorizo and rice and sauté. add the chopped tomato, stock and spices and cook until rice is just about cooked through. Add in mussels to they are cooked through and the peas, spinach and parsley until they are heated.

Cray Cocktail

SERVES 8

This can be an entrée or in spoons as a canape or served on a grazing table or buffet. The crayfish can be cooked and the aioli made the day before the event. Lavender Aioli (recipe from my book The Tasmania Pantry 2 cookbook) also works well in this recipe.

1 large cooked crayfish

lemon aioli

lettuce

cucumber

LEMON AIOLI

2 egg yolks

1 egg

1 tablespoon white vinegar

1 lemon, juice and zest

1 clove garlic

salt and pepper

200ml extra virgin olive oil

To make the aioli, use a blender or food processor to combine the egg yolks, whole egg, vinegar, lemon juice and zest, crushed garlic and a pinch of salt and pepper. While still blending, slowly add the extra virgin olive oil in a steady drizzle to create a thick and creamy emulsion.

Remove the meat from the crayfish tail and body and cut of the legs. Wash and shred the lettuce, slice the cucumber. Assemble the ingredients in an attractive glass and serve

Honey and Soy Chicken Nori Rolls

MAKES 4 LARGE ROLLS

A simple nutritious addition to a children's party but also nice enough for a special occasion canape try prawns or salmon. Rice can be prepared the day before but keep it moist and covered.

1 cup sushi rice

1 tablespoon rice wine vinegar

1 teaspoon caster sugar

4 nori sheets

2 tablespoons mayonnaise

HONEY SOY CHICKEN STRIPS

400 grams chicken thighs

1 tablespoon soy sauce

1 tablespoon honey

1.5 tablespoons corn flour

oil for pan-frying

To cook the rice, place the rice in a colander and rinse under cold running water for a minute to wash off any excess starch. Put the rice into a heavy based saucepan with 1 and ½ cups water. Bring to a gentle boil, reduce the heat and cook covered for about 12 minutes or until all of the water has been absorbed. Remove from the heat and leave to sit for 10 minutes covered to finish cooking. Add the vinegar to the rice and fold through. Spread the rice in a thin layer on to a sheet of baking paper on a board to cool.

To make the filling, slice the chicken into 5ml strips. Mix the honey and soy sauce together in a bowl, add the chicken strips and leave to marinade for a few hours, preferably overnight. Add the cornflour to the chicken and add a dash of oil into the frying pan and fry over a low heat until cooked.

Smoked Salmon Pate

MAKES ABOUT A CUP AND A HALF

This is one of those recipes that's actually so easy it's not really a recipe and is almost embarrassing to include in a cookbook. But then whenever I serve it at a party everyone raves about it and that's what we like. Little effort for a wow factor result. Serve with veggie sticks and bickies I buy the smoked salmon offcuts from the Tassal Salmon Shop Salamanca and have them in the freezer for a quick to whip up dip.

100 grams cream cheese

1 tablespoon mayo (see page 62)

250 grams smoked salmon (I love the Cajun peppered hot smoked)

1 teaspoon dill

Put all ingredients in the blender and whiz together and serve, can be done the day before the event.

Tzatziki Dip

MAKES A FEW CUPS

A dip makes a super cute veggie garden in a little pot for a party. In the picture here I have topped it with a layer of black dyed cooked cous cous for the dirt.

1 cup natural yoghurt
half large cucumber
1 tablespoon dill
2 cloves garlic
salt and pepper
¼ teaspoon cumin

Cut the cucumber in half and scope out the seeds and dice into a small dice. Crush the garlic and mix with the yoghurt, cucumber chopped dill, cumin and then season with salt and pepper.

Lamingtons

MAKES 16

I have managed a first prize for my lamingtons one year at the Bream Creek show! Make your cake a few weeks before the event if you need and freeze to simply ice them on the day of the event or the night before.

120 grams sugar

4 eggs

1 teaspoon vanilla essence

50 grams butter

120 grams self raising flour

25 grams butter

100ml water

500 grams icing sugar

50 grams Dutch processed cocoa

shredded or desiccated coconut to coat

jam – optional

Preheat the oven to 180°C.

To make the cake beat the sugar and eggs and vanilla, beat in melted butter and then fold in the flour. Pour into a lined 20 cm square straight sided cake pan. Bake for around 25 minutes or until golden and cooked through. Cool.

Cut cake into 16 squares and trim sides if feeling fancy (or you are entering in the BCS those CWA judge ladies are fussy). Mix the water and icing sugar and coat together to make a runny icing and then dip each piece of cake in the icing quickly, so it does not soak up too much and then coat in coconut. Slice and fill with a good spread of jam if you are feeling decadent.

Parsley Dip

MAKES A FEW CUPS

I love the use of the leftover bread in Greek dips and most of us will have a few crusts in the freezer.

3 crusts bread
1 cup parsley
1 tablespoon white vinegar
2 cloves garlic
½ small onion
salt and pepper
olive oil

In a food processor blend the bread into crumbs and remove from the blender

Add the parsley, vinegar, garlic, onion and salt and pepper and blend until smooth add the bread and then the oil in a slow drizzle.

Christmas Pudding

MAKES 3 LARGE PUDDINGS

I must give credit for this recipe to Nanna Spaulding. I have adapted it and added measurements I use but this is the recipe we were hunting down for the Bream Creek Farmers market cookbook. We ended up with a couple of the same recipes from different families as so many familes make this pudding! It needs to be continued to be shared. And I have had some very fussy excellent cooking older women love it when I make it! I also make my Christmas cakes on the same day as the puddings, so soak the fruits on the same day. I do not make mine months in advance and I do not dry it out as I have room in the freezer. I would imagine the reasons for drying out the pudding was simply storage. I use oven bags and then pudding cloths for aesthetics but you could flour the pudding cloth well. Steam in a steamer over a large pot still in the cloth for at least an hour to serve.

2 cups brandy

1 cup dry breadcrumbs

2.25 kilos mixed dried fruit

200 grams glace cherries

1 teaspoon cinnamon

200 grams slivered almonds

½ teaspoon allspice

½ nutmeg ground

1 teaspoon lemon essence

1 teaspoon almond essence

1 teaspoon vanilla essence

⅓ cup white sugar

⅓ cup brown sugar

¼ teaspoon salt

160 grams butter

¾ cup treacle

4 eggs

¾ cup cream

310 grams plain flour

¾ teaspoon bicarb

Soak the breadcrumbs, fruits, cherries, spices, essence almonds in the brandy mixed well overnight but ideally for a few days.

Beat the sugars and the butter until light and creamy. Beat in the eggs. Beat in the treacle, salt, flour, cream and bicarb and then mix though the fruits.

Divide the mixture between the three oven bags and tie tightly removing excess air. Wrap in the pudding cloth. Place in a large pot with a plate upturned. I tie the puddings to wooden spoons so the pudding doesn't fill with water and sneak in any gaps where we have tied it. Simmer for 6 hours. Cool and dry or freeze until needed.

To serve steam for at least one hour.

Kahlua Custard

MAKES 800 ML ENOUGH TO SERVE ONE LARGE PUDDING

One year ,after making brandy custard for many years (and I do not even like Brandy) I decided to make a Kahlua custard rather than buying a new bottle of brandy just for the custard. Kahlua custard is a new tradition I will continue with now as its so delicious!

3 eggs
50 grams flour
50 grams sugar
600ml milk
100 grams chocolate
60ml Kahlua

In a pot over a low heat bring the milk to a gentle simmer and turn off. In a large bowl mix the flour, sugar and eggs together and then pour in the milk and Kahlua and mix well. Return to the pot and over a medium heat, bring to a gentle simmer stirring well until thickened and cooked. Serve immediately.

If you have a thermocooker you'll know how to make custard but just put all ingredients in the bowl and cook at 90°C for about 10 minutes on speed 4.

Christmas Fruit Cake

MAKE 2 CAKES

This recipe makes 1 thick 20cm round cake plus one a bit thinner to enjoy with thick butter in the lead up to Christmas.

1 teaspoon nutmeg

1 teaspoon cinnamon

1 ¾ cups sultanas

¼ cup pitted dates

3 cups dried fruits

1 cup glace cherries

1 cup brandy

250 grams butter

1 ½ cups brown sugar

5 eggs

1 teaspoon vanilla

1 ½ cups flour

Soak the nutmeg, cinnamon, sultanas, chopped dates, dried fruits, glace cherries in the brandy for at least overnight.

Preheat the oven to 170°C.

Cream the butter, brown sugar until light and fluffy. Beat in the eggs and vanilla and fold through flour and then mix in the fruits. Line 2 cake tins with baking paper on the base and grease the sides. Distribute the mix through the 2 cake tins. I do one thick to decorate and one thinner to enjoy fresh which will cook quicker.

Bake for 40 minutes or until cooked through. Lower the temperature of the oven if it starts to darken too much.

Turducken

SERVES A LOT

The duck in the middle of the turkey and the chickens actual purpose, is for the fat to render down through the other meats as they cook to keep all the meat moist. So, if you are using a free range unprocessed (not pumped full of chemicals and whatever else to keep them juicy) turkey, duck and chicken then the end result is amazing!

1 whole turkey

1 duck

1 small chicken

STUFFING

½ loaf bread

1 small onion

about 2 tablespoons of each fresh herbs: sage, tarragon, thyme, parsley

1 tablespoon butter

salt and pepper

First step is to bone out all the birds. but leave the wings and leg bone in the turkey to maintain the shape when roasting. Boning poultry is easy and gets better with practice so if you were planning on making one of these turduckens for Christmas, and you have not boned out poultry before, you could practice boning out some chickens in the months leading up to Christmas. This is a more economical way to purchase chicken meat anyway and you have a carcass left to make a lovely stock for a soup. Or ask your butcher to bone the birds out for you.

To bone out the bird have the bird breast side down on the chopping board, cut the skin of the bird along the backbone, and carefully cut down each side of the carcass without piercing the skin and leaving as much meat as possible when taking out the carcass. To make the stuffing, grate the bread into breadcrumbs, finely chop onion and herbs and mix altogether.

Put the turkey skin side down on the board then lay the duck on the turkey and then the chook on the duck, put a strip of stuffing in the chook and then wrap the duck around the chicken and finally the turkey around the duck and sew or tie up.

Turn over so it is breast side up and roast in a 160°C oven. The cooking time is going to vary hugely: size of birds, your ovens, stuffing - if you layer the stuffing between the birds, that will slow down the movement of the hot fat and so slow down the cooking time. Your best bet is to use a meat thermometer in the fattest part of the bird nowhere near a bone, to test when it is cooked. 165°C is cooked, when you find a 165°C spot check a few more spots like the thigh and under the wing to make sure they are all over 165°C then leave it to rest.

I would recommend putting the turducken in a 160°C oven 4 hours before you want to be actually sitting down to eat it. If you end up with mega fatty birds and all the fat heats up and cooks the birds really quickly in a hot 160°C oven in 2 hours, then you can always pull it out to rest, and put it back in a hot oven to heat it back up for the last 20 minutes before serving so the internal temp is back to 165°C before serving if needed.

Cut in half and slice to serve.

Beef Wellington

SERVES 10-15

To make your own puff pastry find a recipe on my website eloiseemmett.com. If you choose to use a packet pastry make sure the pastry is made with butter for the best flavour.

1 piece whole scotch fillet 1.5 -2 kg

1 kilo puff pastry sheets

1 egg

CHICKEN LIVER PATE

500 grams chicken livers

1 tablespoon butter

½ small brown onion

1 clove garlic

2 rashers fatty bacon

30ml brandy

2 tablespoons fresh basil leaves

1 teaspoon thyme leaves

salt and cracked pepper

60ml cream

Preheat the oven to 180°C.

To make the pate sauté the livers, peeled garlic and onion and the roughly chopped bacon in the butter until soft, add the herbs, and cream and simmer for 8 minutes or until the livers are just cooked. Puree and season with the salt and pepper and refrigerate until cooled and set. This can all be done simply in the thermocooker if you have one.

To make the wellington, trim sinew from meat and seal until brown on all sides in a hot pan. Refrigerate until cool. Cover the meat in the pate and wrap with sheets of pastry, using egg wash to seal the pastry and with having minimal patches of thick layers of pastry as this will be take longer to cook and be soggy rather than golden and crisp.

Bake in a 180°C oven for about 40 minutes to 1 hour to be cooked to medium. Use a meat thermometer for the best results and it will be best left to rest for at least 20 minutes (be mindful that it will continue cooking in this time). Slice and serve

Herb, Garlic and Fetta Bread Roll Christmas Tree

SERVES A BIG GROUP

Fun and delicious!

750 grams bakers flour

1.5 teaspoons sugar

1.5 teaspoons salt

1.5 teaspoons yeast

450-500ml lukewarm water

2-3 tablespoons of your best robust extra virgin olive oil

sea salt

2 big sprigs rosemary

8 sage leaves

4 cloves garlic

20 cherry tomatoes

To make the bread dough, in your mixer with the dough hook your thermocooker or with strong arms knead the flour, sugar, salt, yeast and water together well until it's a smooth dough. 2 minutes in the thermocooker or about 15 minutes by hand on the bench. Leave to rise and double in size.

Preheat the oven to 200°C

Knock the dough back by kneading it and cut into 36 pieces. Roll into tight balls and assemble on a baking tray lined with baking paper so the balls are just touching in the shape of a Christmas tree. Sit the cherry tomatoes on the dough, the chopped herbs and finely chopped garlic, drizzle with the oil and sprinkle on the sea salt. Bake for around 25 minutes or until golden brown and cooked through.

Lamb Mexican Meatballs

MAKES 20-30 TABLESPOON SIZE MEAT BALLS

500 grams lamb mince

1 onion

2 cloves garlic

1 tablespoon oregano

1 tablespoon smoked paprika

1 tablespoon cumin

fresh or dried chilli to taste

1 egg

1 cup fresh bread crumbs

TO SERVE

salsa, guacamole, cheese and corn chips to serve (optional)

Dice onion, crush garlic and mix all ingredients together well. Roll into balls and pan fry in a large heavy based pan over a medium heat until cooked through. Serve hot or cold with a dipping salsa or with corn chips, salsa and guacamole.

Cheviche, Sashimi, Carpaccio, Tartare Fresh Fish

When you have super fresh seafood then this is the best way to serve it. With the added bonus of it being very easy, its great starter for a dinner party when you have something a little bit tricky to cook for your main. But it has to be fresh! Try oysters, scallops, fresh white fish, tuna, salmon. It can also be arranged on a platter or in small serving spoons as a canape.

Pick any of the following ingredients from the list below. Get creative!

RAW FRESH SEAFOOD

(80-100 grams fresh fish per person)

oysters

salmon

scallops

tuna

ACIDS

lemon juice

lime juice

vinegar

VEGETABLES

capers

pickled vegetables like gherkins

OILS

sesame oil

extra virgin olive oil

lemon agrumato

flavoured oils

SAUCES

soy

OTHER

fresh herbs shredded

sesame seeds

sea salt and pepper

The styles are all quite similar, but here is my take on what they are:

- Carpaccio is fresh fish of choice, sliced as thin as possible, arranged on a platter with the topping sprinkled over.
- Tartare is fresh fish of choice, cut into a 5 mm dice, mixed with the ingredients and served together.
- Cheviche is sliced fresh fish of choice, arranged on a platter. Some will leave this to marinade to cook through in the acid.
- Sashimi is 3 mm sliced fresh fish of choice, arranged on the platter.

Here are some ideas, but its limitless what you can do:

- Salmon with soy sauce, rice wine vinegar, sesame oil and toasted sesame seeds
- Oysters with capers, gherkins, red wine vinegar and robust extra virgin olive oil
- Scallops with lime, capers and pomegranate vinegar

Carpaccio, Tartare Red Meat

When you have beautiful produce to start with it will always require less work. I would pick a carpaccio to serve as an entree when my main requires a little fussing. Have everything else ready for the dish before the event such as the parmesan shaved and the capers diced.

Pick any of the following ingredients from the list below. Get creative!

RAW FRESH RED MEAT

(80-100 grams fresh meat per person)

wallaby

lamb

venison

ACIDS

lemon juice

lime juice

vinegar

VEGETABLES

capers

pickled vegetables like gherkins

OILS

sesame oil

extra virgin olive oil

lemon agrumato

truffle oil

SAUCES

soy

ponzu

OTHER

parmesan or other strong flavoured cheese like goats cheese

fresh herbs shredded

sesame seeds

sea salt and pepper

grisisni sticks or croutons

The styles are quite similar, but here is my take on what they are:

- Carpaccio is raw meat of choice, sliced as thin as possible, arranged on a platter with the topping sprinkled over.
- Tartare is raw meat of choice, cut into a 5 mm dice, mixed with the ingredients and served together.

Here are some ideas, but its limitless what you can do:

- Wallaby fillet with parmesan cheese, tuffle oil, basil, pepper and robust extra virgin olive oil.
- Lamb with soy sauce, sesame oil and rice wine vinegar.
- Venison with capers, gherkins, red wine vinegar and extra virgin olive oil.

Sandwich, Wrap and Open Sandwich Ideas

With the right ingredients little open sandwiches can look quite fancy for a formal canape with the bread a good filler to soak up the booze, if that's something you think the group you are entertaining will need. Little pieces of baguette tied with twine look super cute at a picnic. Cucumber sandwiches can be served at a formal high tea and sandwiches and wraps are great for children's parties. Fairy bread- white bread, butter and sprinkles is always the kids favourite and easy and economical to make.

OPEN SANDWICH

tomato, basil aioli

ham and mustard

salami and cheese

pastrami

smoked salmon and cream cheese

roast eggplant, capsicum, zucchini and olive

SANDWICH

cucumber

salmon and cucumber

ham and cheese

curried egg

WRAP

chilli chicken mayo

pesto chicken

lamb and tzatziki

Lamb Sausage Roll

MAKES 2 DOZEN SMALL ROLLS

500 grams lamb mince

2 onions

4 cloves garlic

2 large sprigs rosemary

2 tablespoons thyme

1 teaspoon smoked paprika

¼ teaspoon cumin

2 eggs (one for egg wash)

1 cup fresh breadcrumbs

5 sheets puff pastry

Preheat the oven to 180°C.

Peel and dice the onion, crush the garlic and mix in a large bowl with the chopped rosemary and thyme, paprika, cumin, mince, one egg and breadcrumbs.

Lay the pastry sheets out and cut in half. Pipe or carefully lay the mince down one side of the pastry length ways. Egg wash the other side and roll up, repeat with all the pastry and mince. Cut into length into 8 rolls and lay on a baking tray. Cook for around 20 minutes or until golden brown and cooked through.

Beef and Veggie Pie with a Cauliflower Top

SERVES 8

Who doesn't love a good pie! Serve one of these delicious meat and veg filled pies at the kids party and there will be hardly any room left in the bellies for all the treats.

1 tablespoon extra virgin olive oil

1 onion

2 garlic cloves

1 large carrot

2 sticks celery

1 kilogram beef mince

4 tablespoons plain flour

1 ½ cups beef/chicken stock

4 tablespoons tomato paste

2 tablespoons Worcestershire sauce

1 tablespoon soy sauce

½ teaspoon rosemary

½ teaspoon thyme

1 cup peas

1 egg

PASTRY

400 grams plain flour

200 grams butter

pinch salt

100ml water

CAULIFLOWER LID

½ cauliflower

1 tablespoon butter

60 grams cheddar cheese

Preheat the oven to 190°C.

Finely dice the onion and carrot (to ½ cm size dice) and crush the garlic. Heat the oil in a large heavy based pan over a medium heat and then sauté the diced onion, carrots and garlic for about 2-3 minutes until soft. Add the beef mince and cook for a further 15-20 minutes until the meat has completely browned. Stir in the flour, then add the stock, tomato paste, Worcestershire sauce, soy sauce and dried herbs. Cover and cook for a further 20-25 minutes. Season with salt and pepper, add the cooked peas and then cool.

To make the pastry, in a large bowl with your hands rub the salt and butter into the flour until it resembles fine crumbs. Mix the water into the flour to make the pastry dough, and then rest the dough for at least ½ hour before rolling. Meanwhile grease the base and sides of 8 small pie dishes. Once the pastry has rested, roll it to approximately 5mm thick and then place the pastry into the base and sides of each of the pie dishes.

To make the cauliflower topping cut cauliflower into florets and steam for around 10 minutes or until cooked through and puree with the butter in a blender while still hot, season with salt and pepper.

Add the cooled beef mixture into the pie dishes and then top with cauliflower and cheese.

Bake for about 25 minutes or until golden brown and cooked through.

Crayfish Omelette

SERVES 4

6 eggs

2 spring onions

3 sprigs tarragon

100ml cream

salt

pepper

50 grams cheese

butter

½ cooked crayfish

Heat butter in a heavy based frying pan and saute the finely chopped spring onions. Crack the eggs into a bowl and add the cream and whisk together well with a pinch of salt and pepper.

Pour eggs into pan while the butter is hot and sizzling. Sprinkle chopped tarragon, crayfish meat and grated cheese and lower heat until the omelette is cooked through.

You can transfer to the oven to finish cooking.

RANNOCH QUAIL

Grilled Rannoch Quail with Walnut and Blue Cheese

SERVES 4 FOR AN ENTREE

This combination is always a hit with my workshop guests. I love Tasmanian honey and I always use fresh extra virgin olive oil when making my own salad dressings. The fresher the oil the better it is for us. Try different cheeses and nuts, a sharp parmesan will work well. Fresh in season walnuts are pretty hard to pass on though.

2-4 large boned butterflied quail

extra virgin olive oil for cooking

DRESSING

20ml apple cider vinegar

1 tablespoon honey

1 tablespoon Dijon mustard

40ml extra virgin olive oil

SALAD

100 grams blue cheese

100 grams walnuts

2 apples

2 cups salad leaves

To make the dressing, mix ingredients well to together.

To cook the quail, in a pan or the flat grill of the BBQ, cook the quail in a dash of extra virgin olive oil for around 4 minutes on each side or until cooked through.

To make the salad, roughly chops walnuts and cheese and slice the apples, toss with ¾ of the salad dressing. Add the leaves and serve with the quail with the remaining dressing poured on top.

Petuna Salmon Glazed with Lemon Myrtle and Honey

SERVES 8

A side of salmon makes a stunning centre piece for a plated buffet style event. Salmon is a forgiving fish to cook in bulk as it handles being overcooked and delicious undercooked, room for mistakes when busy.

1 side Petuna salmon
3 tablespoons honey
1 tablespoon extra virgin olive oil
1 tablespoon lime juice
½ teaspoon cumin
1 teaspoon ground lemon myrtle
cracked pepper
sea salt

DRESSING

3 tablespoons light soy sauce
2 tablespoons lime juice
1 tablespoon honey
fresh chilli to taste

SALAD

1 cucumber
2 carrots
2 cup red cabbage
2 cup lettuce
2 spring onion
½ bunch coriander
sprigs of mint

Preheat the oven to 160°C.

In a bowl place the honey, oil, lime juice, cumin, lemon myrtle, sea salt and pepper and mix well.

Lay the salmon on a tray lined with baking paper and coat well with half the marinade. Place the tray in the oven after 15 minutes. Coat the salmon with the remaining marinade and bake for a further 10 minutes or until the salmon is cooked how you like it.

Mix the dressing ingredients together, slice the salad ingredients and mix well with the dressing and serve with the hot salmon.

Eclairs

MAKES 40 SMALL PUFFS OR 20 SMALL ECLAIRS

A classic and so many different ideas of ways we can serve eclairs, this is one of my favourite desserts. We had white chocolate and raspberry cream mini eclairs on my Mussel Boy's menu. I simply layered profiteroles out on a board to spell Maggie for her birthday rather than tackling a crocombe bush on the day of an event! One little hint I find is that when trying to double or triple the recipe it never seems to work well so even if I am making loads I will make this smaller batch a few times rather than doubling it. Make the eclair pastry the day before or a few days before the event. They also make a delicious savoury canape filled with pate or dip, salmon and cream cheese or even warmed with cheeses. So many different uses for an entree, dessert or canape.

250ml water

100 gram butter

pinch salt

1 teaspoon sugar

135 grams plain flour

3 large eggs

300 grams chocolate

300ml cream

2 tablespoon icing sugar

Preheat the oven to 210°C.

In a heavy based pot bring the water to the boil over a low heat is the butter is melted by the time it boils. Add flour, sugar and salt and beat well, cooking over a low heat until the mixture is smooth and leaves the side of the pan.

Cool slightly and transfer to your mixer or thermocooker and beat in one egg one at a time.

Pipe the pastry onto lined baking trays and bake for around 15 minutes or until golden brown and cooked through. Cool.

Melt chocolate by placing it in a stainless steel bowl that fits on top of a pot. Put water in the pot and simmer and gently melt the chocolate and dip each eclair in to coat the top layer.

Whip the cream with the icing sugar and when the chocolate is set cut the eclair in half and pipe the cream in.

Quiche

MAKES 12 MINI QUICHES

This is s simple recipe my kids love, so its great for a children's party. Quiches are also a nice choice for a adult canape and you can try so many different fillings like roast pumpkin, goats cheese and caramelised onion or beetroot and fetta or spicy chorizo and cheddar to make them fancy.

1 sheet puff pastry

½ onion

1 clove garlic

1 small carrot

1 rasher bacon

3 tablespoon tomato

½ teaspoon basil

½ teaspoon oregano

½ cup peas

2 eggs

¼ cup cream

100 grams tasty cheese

Preheat the oven to 180°C.

Crush the garlic, finely dice the onion, carrot and bacon, saute in a dash of extra virgin olive oil in a heavy based pan over a medium heat until soft. Add the crushed tomato and herbs and season with salt and pepper.

Crack the eggs into a bowl and whisk well with the cream.

Cut the pastry and line the base of greased mini quiche tin - prick the pastry with a fork. Add a tablespoon of filling in each and pour in egg mix. Top with grated cheese.

Bake in a 180°C oven for about 20 minutes or until golden and cooked.

Caramel Macadamia Pie

SERVES 10

BASE

180 grams butter

240 grams plain flour

3 tablespoons water

1 tablespoon sugar

FILLING

4 eggs

250ml golden syrup

60 grams brown sugar

60 grams caster sugar

30 grams butter

90 grams macadamia nuts

TOPPING

75 grams brown sugar

3 tablespoons honey

45 grams butter

150 grams macadamia nuts

To make the base, in a mixing bowl (or the food processor) rub the butter into the flour and sugar, then mix in water. Grease and flour a 20cm tart, flan or cake tin. Roll the pastry out to line the tin and leave to rest for at least 30 minutes.

To make the filling, chop 90 grams of the macadamia nuts up in to smaller pieces and mix well with all the other ingredients. Pour into the pastry and bake for 20 minutes until it is just cooked.

Meanwhile for the topping, cut 150 grams of macadamia nuts in half and put in a pot with the honey, butter and brown sugar and cook on a low heat for about three minutes, pour on top of the pie and bake for about 10 minutes until golden.

Toffee Apples

MAKES 12

12 apples

12 sticks

¼ cup water

1 cups sugar

1 teaspoon vinegar

To make the toffee, in a heavy based pot over a low heat, simmer the sugar, vinegar and water. Do not stir and keep it to the lowest heat possible. It will take 10-15 minutes to start to caramelise and turn a golden brown, keep a careful eye on it or it will burn quickly.

Put the sticks in the apples and dip in the toffee and leave to cool and set.

RANNOCH QUAIL

Rannoch Quail Baked with Bacon and Tarragon

SERVES 4 FOR A MAIN

I have been a lover of Rannoch Quail well before I moved to the Tasman Peninsula 20 years ago where it was a local business and dropped at my kitchen door from the farm when I needed it. This is an easy and delicious one tray bake, prep it before your guests arrive, even the day before to simply put in the oven.

4 large partially boned quail

4 rashers bacon

1 tablespoon extra virgin olive oil

6 cloves garlic

8 shallots or small brown onions

8 small potatoes

4 long sprigs tarragon

2 teaspoons butter

salt and pepper

400 grams green beans

Preheat the oven to 180°C.

To prepare the quail rub both sides of it with butter, season with salt and pepper, lay the tarragon inside the quail and wrap the quail up in bacon. Lay the birds in a baking dish with the peeled garlic cloves, scrubbed pink eye potatoes and a dash of extra virgin olive oil.

Bake for 35 minutes or until the birds are cooked through. Top and tail the beans and throw them in the pan coated with a dash of extra virgin olive oil for the last 8 minutes of cooking.

Green Peppercorn Wallaby Fillet, Roast Capsicum, Eggplant and Horseradish Cream

SERVES 4

4 wallaby fillets 600-800 grams

2 tablespoons green peppercorns

2 red capsicum

1 large zucchini

1 eggplant

2 cups spinach

100 grams mushrooms

4 cloves garlic

1 tablespoon horseradish paste

150ml cream

100 grams haloumi

flour to dust

extra virgin olive oil for cooking

Preheat the oven to 200°C.

Crush the peppercorns and rub over the wallaby fillets and set aside. Place the capsicum on a baking tray and rub with a little extra virgin olive oil. Bake capsicum in the over until brown/black. Cool and peel off skin and remove seeds. Slice into 1 cm strips. Place mushrooms on tray and bake in oven with a dash of oil and garlic cloves.

Slice eggplant into 5ml slice and rub in a little salt leave for one hour and wash well. This will help remove some bitterness. Slice the zucchini in a 5mm slice. BBQ or Grill or even bake in the oven the eggplant and zucchini with a little oil until cooked . Slice into 1cm strips. Cool and mix the veggies together, serve cold or warm tossed with the spinach.

Whip the cream and mix in the horseradish and season with salt and pepper.

To cook the Wallaby grill on the BBQ or in a pan for around 4 minutes on each side medium rare. To cook the haloumi, roll slices in flour and add to the pan or BBQ for a minuite on each side. Rest the wallaby for around 10 minutes wrapped in foil to keep warm and serve with the salad and cream

Beetroot and Goats Cheese Salad

SERVES 4-6 AS A SIDE

4 large beetroot

2 cups spinach leaves

100 grams goats chevre or soft goats cheese

basil leaves

robust extra virgin olive oil

sea salt

cracked pepper

Preheat the oven to 180°C.

Rub the beetroot in a little oil and bake for around 20 minutes or until cooked through, they have little resistance when poked with a fork or skewer. Leave them to cool and then peel.

Dice the beetroot in a 1.5cm dice or a slice and arrange with the spinach, goats cheese, ripped basil leaves, drizzle with the extra virgin olive oil and season with sea salt and pepper.

BBQ Octopus with Baked Haloumi and Olives

SERVES 4-6 AS A MAIN

1 kilo octopus tenatcles/leg

6 cloves garlic

extra virgin olive oil

2 tablespoon oregano

white pepper

TO SERVE

100 grams haloumi cheese

80 grams olives

6 bay leaves

3 tablespoons oregano

extra virgin olive oil or lemon agrumato

lemon

cracked pepper

sea salt

To prepare the occy remove the skin from the back of each leg. Crush the garlic and mix with a good pinch of white pepper and the oregano and oil. Leave to marinate for a few hours.

Preheat the oven to 180°C.

Drizzle oil in the bottom of a baking serving dish and lay out thin slices of haloumi, the bay leaves, olives and top with the oregano. Drizzle with the oil and zest from the lemon and season well with the salt and pepper. Bake for around 15 minutes until cooked.

To cook the octopus, cook over a medium high heat on the BBQ, Grill or in a pan on the stove top until cooked through. Serve sliced on top of the cheese and olives and drizzle over the juice from the lemon.

Warm Garlicky Potato Salad

SERVES 4-6 FOR A SIDE

I love this simple salad to prepare in a large or small amount. It can go on the side of a lamb on the spit or on the side of a steak or piece of fish on the BBQ. Best made in summer with freshly dug spuds and when our home grown tomatoes are in abundance.

500 grams pink eye potatoes or another waxy variety

6 garlic cloves

extra virgin olive oil

200 grams tomatoes

2 cups spinach leaves

DRESSING

2 tablespoons balsamic vinegar

3 tablespoons extra virgin olive oil

sea salt

cracked pepper

Preheat the oven to 180°C.

Scrub the potatoes and cut if large to a 2cm size and lay on a baking tray, smash the garlic cloves and add to the tray and coat them well with the oil. Bake in the oven for around 25 minutes until crisp and cooked through.

Mix the olive oil and balsamic together to make the dressing. While still hot toss through the tomatoes that have been roughly chopped into a 2 cm dice and the spinach leaves. Dress with the dressing and serve.

Tassal Smoked Salmon and Corn Fritters

MAKES 20-30 SMALL CANAPES

Even though it may be a party it is still nice to consume some actual nutrients and a few veggies.

2 corn cobs (or 2 cups kernels)

1 cup self-raising flour

1 small onion

2 tablespoons dill

2 cloves garlic

1 egg

½ cup milk

1 teaspoon extra virgin olive oil

1 teaspoon butter

salt and pepper

TO SERVE

200 grams Tassal smoked salmon

greens like spinach leaves

cream fraiche

salmon pearls or cavier if available

To make the batter for the fritters, measure the flour into a large bowl. Finely dice the onion and crush the garlic and add to the bowl along with the dill, egg and milk. Mix well and season with salt and pepper. Next, blanch the corn in boiling water for two minutes and then cool. Cut the kernels off the cob and add the corn kernels to the batter and combine.

Heat the oil and butter in a heavy based pan. Scoop heaped tablespoons of the mixture and gently drop one at a time into the pan. Cook until they are golden brown on both sides and cooked through. Allow approximately 2-3 minutes each side.

Serve the corn cakes cool, hot or warm topped with the salmon.

Honey Soy Marinated Fish and Noodles

SERVES 4

Cooking some stir fried veggies and noodles is not at all hard but if you are cooking this noodle box to serve at a large function for example 150 people at a wedding, it might be easier to substitute for a salad that can be pre-prepared (see page 126). These noodle boxes are a bit of a fun novelty for a kids party and at least we know we have got something nutritious in their little bellies.

2 cloves garlic

2 tablespoons light soy sauce

1 tablespoon honey

1 tablespoon extra virgin olive oil

600 grams fish

3 tablespoons cornflour

2 tablespoons extra virgin olive oil

2 cloves garlic

small chilli - optional

¼ cabbage

2 carrots

4 spring onions

bunch bok choy

(add other crispy stir fryable veggies you like)

1 cup noodles (cooked rice noodles, fried noodles or mixture of both)

2 tablespoons sweet soy sauce

To prepare the fish, crush the garlic and mix with the soy sauce, honey and 1 tablespoon of extra virgin olive oil. Cut the fish into pieces, add to the mixture and leave to marinate for at least 2 hours, or preferably overnight.

When you are ready to cook the dish, remove the fish pieces from the marinade and roll each piece in the cornflour. Heat 2 tablespoons of extra virgin olive oil in a large frying pan over medium heat, and fry the fish pieces until cooked through and golden brown.

Peel and crush garlic, slice spring onion and chili, carrot, cabbage and bok choy. Cook the noodles to the packet instructions.

Heat a wok or pan, saute the garlic, onion and carrot. Add the other veg to the pan moving them around in the pan until they are cooked through add the noodles and sauce and serve.

Chicken Noodle Salad

SERVES 4-6

The chicken can be substituted with pork, roast chicken, hot smoked salmon or salmon steaks that have been baked and cooled. Loads of different meals can go in the noodle box. The sichuan pork or Asian schnitzel from the Packed cookbook would also be delicious enough for a fancy event but easy enough to have pre made. The noodle box is fun for a kids party but also a good choice for an evening cocktail canape style party. They would be great for even a formal wedding where nibbles are handed out for a few hours first then something a bit more substantial that can be eaten while standing, without the bother of setting a table and chair for every guest.

1 small chicken

2 cloves garlic

1 knob ginger

1 onion

1 cup soy sauce

1 cup white wine

1 tablespoon sugar

SALAD

1 cup cabbage

2 carrot

8 spring onion

1 cup rice noodles

½ cup fried noodles

10 leaves Vietnamese mint or mint

fresh chilli (optional)

DRESSING

2 tablespoons light soy sauce

½ tablespoon sesame oil

2 tablespoon white vinegar

1 tablespoon extra virgin olive oil

1 teaspoon honey

In a large pot put the water, garlic, ginger, onion, soy sauce, white wine and sugar and bring to the boil. Simmer for 20 minutes to infuse the stock and add the chicken, simmer for 25 minutes or until the chicken is pretty much cooked through. Turn off, leave with the lid on tight until it cools down and it will continue to cook through. Or simply put it all in the slow cooker for around 3 hours. Refrigerate until cold.

Mix all the ingredients for the dressing together.

Shred the cabbage and finely slice the carrot and then cut into thin strips, slice the spring onions, cook the rice noodles in boiling water for about two minutes and cool, slice the mint. Toss all the salad ingredients with the dressing and chicken and serve.

Have the salad chopped, the noodles cooked, the dressing made the chicken cooked in advance to throw together with the crispy noodles to serve easily.

Tassal Salmon One Tray Bake Rice Pilaf

SERVES 2 TO 4

This is a gorgeous one tray dish for a dinner party but will become a weeknight favourite too. I really love salmon for entertaining as it is a very forgivable fish to cook. It can be served raw to well done and due to the oily content, even over cooked fish will still taste great.

2 large fat middle pieces Tassal salmon (approximately 500 grams)

1 tablespoon extra virgin olive oil

1 bunch baby carrots

100 grams chorizo sausage

½ fennel bulb

1 onion

1 clove garlic

1 bay leaf

½ teaspoon cumin

1 teaspoon dill

1 teaspoon tarragon

1 teaspoon smoked paprika

½ cup basmati rice

pinch black pepper

1 cup fish or chicken stock

Preheat the oven to 180°C.

In a deep sided oven and stove proof pan with a lid heat the olive oil and saute the finely sliced onion, fennel, crushed garlic, peeled carrots, diced chorizo and herbs and spices, until onion is soft. Add rice and continue stirring, add stock and stir. Place salmon steaks on top and put the lid on. Transfer to oven and bake for 16 minutes.

Remove from oven and rest with the lid on to finish cooking if needed and serve.

CAMPO DE FLORI LAVENDER

Plum and Campo De Flori Lavender Crème Brulee

SERVES 6

Brulee with any seasonal fruit is always delicious. The key to a good brulee is cooking it slowly at a low temperture, so take this into account when planning. Maybe it is best to cook it the day before and serve it cold if your oven will be busy on the day? Do not be shy with your sprinkle of sugar, a nice thick toffee on top os always good and take your time with the blow torch, I find waving it over in circles works well so there are no burnt bits.

200 grams plums

½ teaspoon dried Campo de Flori lavender

1 cup cream

1 cup milk

⅓ cup sugar

vanilla bean split

3 eggs

Preheat the oven to 150°C

Put the milk and cream in a heavy based pot, split the vanilla bean and scrap into the milk and cream and bring to a gentle simmer, add the lavender. Remove from heat.

Beat the eggs and the sugar in a large bowl until creamy and beat in the hot milk and cream. Beat well.

Cut the plum on the pip and in half and place at the base of the brulee mould you want to use, 6 small or one large, and pour the cream and milk mix on top.

Put the moulds into a water bath in a roasting tray the water should come at least ⅔ of the way up the sides of the moulds, bake for about 30 minutes at 150°C or until set and cooked.

Cool. Sprinkle with sugar and caramelize the sugar with a blow torch and serve

Jelly

SERVES 4-6

200 grams blackberries

500ml apple juice

2 tablespoons gelatine

Put half the apple juice in the blender and the berries and blend. Strain. Bring the other half of the juice to the boil and dissolve the gelatine and mix in with the berry mix and strain again. Put into moulds and leave to set.

Pear and Apple Blackberry Pie

SERVES 6-8

Seriously the easiest sweet pastry recipe ever. All my workshop guests love this recipe. I find finding a gorgeous dish that looks beautiful on the table is the best way to serve it, rather than having the pressure of trying to make it look perfect and removing it from the pie dish to serve.

PASTRY

2 cups self-raising flour

¼ cup icing sugar

125 grams butter

½ cup milk

1 egg white

1 tablespoon caster sugar

FILLING

4 apples

1 punnet blackberries

1 tablespoon corn flour

Preheat the oven to 180°C.

To make the pastry, in a bowl or the food processor blend or mix, flour with the icing sugar and butter until it is like fine crumbs, then mix in the milk. Put on a floured bench roll out ⅔ of the pastry for the base and sides of a 20 cm pie dish and the other ⅓ rolled out for the lid. Leave to rest for at least 20 minutes.

To make the filling, peel and dice ,into 1cm pies, the apple and put in a pot with about 1 tablespoon of water and cook until the apple is cooked but firm. Cool. Toss berries in the corn flour and mix with the apple mix and fill pie. Stick lid to base with the egg white and egg white the top and sprinkle with caster sugar. Put a hole in the top for steam and bake for about 25 minutes.

Coconut Cream and Raspberry Clafoutis

SERVES 4-6

This is a beautiful variation of the classic dish made with cream. It can be made with all sorts of fresh or preserved fruits. A beautiful addition to a summer brunch and easy to put together quickly, can be made in cute little individual ramekins too.

100 grams almond meal

½ teaspoon baking powder

4 eggs

2 tablespoons honey

400ml coconut cream

250 grams raspberries

Preheat the oven to 190°C.

Lay the berries in a ceramic baking dish.

Whisk together all other ingredients well and pour into the baking dish. Transfer dish to oven and bake for around 30 minutes until golden and cooked through.

Skordallia

MAKES 1 CUP

The humble spud has never tasted so good!

250 grams potatoes

60ml white wine vinegar

sea salt

pepper

3 cloves garlic

1 tablespoon lemon juice

100ml extra virgin olive oil

Peel and dice the potato and put it into a pot and cover with water, bring to the boil and cook for 15-20 minutes until cooked through. Strain and cool. In the food processor or the thermocooker blend the potato, garlic, salt, pepper, vinegar, olive oil and lemon juice until smooth.

RANNOCH QUAIL

Miso Grilled Rannoch Quail

SERVES 4

When making this for a entree for a large group try the Ranch Farm quail breasts.

2-4 large quail
2 tablespoons white miso paste
400 grams sweet potato
6 spring onions
2 cups spinach leaves
chilli oil

Rub the miso paste over the birds and leave for at least an hour.

Preheat the oven to 180°C.

Peel and dice into a 1cm dice the sweet potato, coat in a dash of extra virgin olive oil and lay in a baking tray. Bake for around 25 minutes or until cooked through. Chop the spring onions into a 5mm chunk and add coat in a dash of extra virgin olive oil and add to the sweet potato for the last 5 minutes of cooking.

To cook the quail, in a pan or the flat grill of the BBQ, cook the quail in a dash of extra virgin olive oil for around 4 minutes on each side or until cooked through.

Serve the quail hot with the sweet potato, onion and spinach. Dress with the chilli oil.

BREAM CREEK VINEYARD

RECIPE ADAPTED FROM ANA PIMENTA MEAT YOUR BEEF FARM TOURS RECIPE

Bream Creek Pinot Double Cooked Beef

SERVES 10-12 GENEROUSLY

Credit for this amazing recipe goes to Ana from Meat your Beef Farm Tours on King Island. I have adapted her recipe from The first Tasmania Pantry Cookbook. The original recipe has been a hit all the times I have cooked it since the book was published. All the hard work is done the days leading up to the event so it is easy to serve on the day. This one works well for a big group like Christmas day! This adaption was stumbled on when I had a gluten free guest at a weekend cooking retreat at Little Norfolk Bay Events and Chalets and only realised at the last minute that stout is not gluten free, so went with the Pinot Noir substitute. Delicious!

2 large onions

4 celery sticks

4 carrots

half chuck of beef (approximately 2.5 kilograms)

3 tablespoons extra virgin olive oil bay leaves

20 black peppercorns

2 litres beef stock

100ml honey

1 bottle Bream Creek Pinot Noir

extra virgin olive oil

butter

mashed potatoes and greens to serve

To cook the beef, roughly dice the onions, celery and carrots into 2cm pieces. Remove the beef from the refrigerator, bring to room temperature and cut into 2 long pieces. Heat the oil in a large, heavy-based saucepan over medium heat, add the onions, celery, carrots, bay leaves and peppercorns, and sauté for 5 minutes, or until the vegetables start to colour. Remove the vegetables from the pan and seal the beef on all sides. Remove from the pan.

Preheat the oven to 150°C.

Tip vegetables into a very large, heavy-based saucepan (or two saucepans if you don't have a big enough one) and place the beef on top of the vegetables. Pour over the beef stock, honey and wine, cover with a lid and cook in the oven for 4-5 hours, or until the beef is very tender. Remove from the oven and let cool to room temperature.

Remove beef from the saucepan. Tip the vegetables and cooking liquid through a colander, reserving the liquid. Lay a large rectangle of plastic wrap on the bench. Place the beef on top and roll the beef into a tight cylinder shape, using the plastic wrap to help you form a very tight roll. Refrigerate overnight.

The following day, pour the cooking liquid into a small saucepan, bring to a simmer over low heat and reduce by ¾ - this will take a hour or so and make a delicious sauce for the beef.

Preheat the oven to 160°C.

Remove the beef from the fridge, take off the plastic wrap and cut into slices around 3-4cm thick. Heat a little olive oil and butter in an oven proof frying pan over medium heat and brown the beef slices for one minute on each side. Transfer to the oven and cook for 10 minutes.

Serve the beef with mashed potatoes, greens and the beef reduction sauce.

Cheese Ball Christmas Tree

SERVES A LOT

A popular party favourite that can be made with all sorts of cheese, nut and meat combinations. Fun at Christmas made into an antipasto Christmas tree!

CHEESE BALL

250 grams cream cheese

60 grams parmesan

60 grams mozzeralla

1 cloves garlic

½ cup fresh herbs such as parsley, rosemary, thyme

1 tablespoon sour cream

TO SERVE

biscuits

cured meats

olives

fresh herbs

sundried tomatoes

Chop garlic and herbs and blend all ingredients together well for the cheese ball.

Decorate with antipasto ingredients for a Christmas tree, such as cured meats, olives, fresh herbs and sundried tomatoes.

Slow Cooked Lamb

SERVES A LOT

Using a gas spit roast is actually a pretty easy way to cook lamb for the big event, and really delicious too. Otherwise lining up electric slow cookers is a fairly fail safe way to prepare a heap of lamb for a large party. Cooking over fire is always fun and if you are confident in your ability that's great but I prefer to do my fire cooking while relaxing at camping not to prepare a meal for an important event and I like the control that gas and electricity provide. Always make sure your meat is ready a few hours before you want to eat as resting it is important anyway but if for any reason there is a mistake you will have that extra time. Not all slow cookers cook at the same temperature but the owner of the slow cooker will know how it works. A rough guide is one 2.5 kilo leg of lamb for 15 people. One large leg of lamb will fit in a large slow cooker. Or use baking trays in the oven. Easy and delicious!

leg of lamb

2 bulbs garlic

2 brown onions

rosemary

thyme

pepper

salt

Cut a garlic bulb in half through the middle and put in the bottom of the slow cooker and slice an onion, put lamb on top with a handful of rosemary and thyme, sprinkle with salt and pepper and cook in the slow cooker for about 6 hours and the meat falls of the bone.

The lamb will make an impressive meal served with the warm garlicky potato salad (see page 120) or in fresh rolls and gravy or couscous salad or in a beautiful wrap with salad and tzatziki as a souvlaki.

PORT ARTHUR LAVENDER

Lemon and Port Arthur Lavender Tart

SERVES 8

Make one large tart or 8 small in muffin holders

BASE

240 grams plain flour
1 tablespoon sugar
180 grams butter
2 tablespoons water

FILLING

4 medium lemons
6 eggs
100 grams sugar
100ml cream
10 drops Port Arthur Lavender oil

Preheat the oven to 180°C.

Use a food processor to make the pastry base. Tip the flour and sugar into the processor, add the cubed butter and pulse until the mixture resembles fine breadcrumbs. With the motor running, add the water and blend until the mixture comes together into a firm dough.

Grease a 20cm tart tin and sprinkle with flour. Roll the pastry out on a floured bench and line the base and sides of the tin, then set aside to rest for at least 30 minutes.

To make the filling, zest and juice the lemons, and beat with the eggs, sugar, lavender and cream until well combined. Pour into the pastry base and bake for 30 minutes, or until the filling is set.

Remove from the oven and set aside to cool before serving.

Hummus

SERVES PLENTY

200 grams cooked chickpeas

5 cloves garlic

approximately 100ml robust extra virgin olive oil

juice of 2 lemons

sea salt

pepper

1 teaspoon smoked paprika

SERVING IDEA FOR A PLATED BUFFET

lamb cutlets or koftas

fetta cheese

olives

extra virgin olive oil

parsley

Place all the ingredients in the thermocooker or blender. Blend together to form a smooth paste.

Season well with salt and pepper.

Additional Recipes

I have not included recipes from my other books to keep these recipes fresh and new. You will find over 300 recipes in my other books that would be incredible for entertaining which I have cooked over many occasions.

The Real Food for Kids Cookbook includes great choices for kids parties and other occasions like: banana bread, carrot cake, pasties, kiss biscuits, apple cakes, scones, tea cakes, coconut loaf and more.

Seafood Everyday has loads of entertaining recipes, a dozen oyster recipes, crayfish, my famous seafood chowder, and many others that are great for any party.

The Tasmania Pantry 1 & 2 both contain loads of recipes for some of Tasmania's best ingredients like octopus and wallaby and you will find plenty of recipes for entertaining in them.

As mentioned earlier in the book, my *Packed* cookbook has some great recipes for picnics or noodle box mini meals and recipes for other occasions.

My books are fully produced in Tasmania and printed in Australia. They have also have been awarded 6 cookbook awards. Order online at www.eloiseemmett.com and we will post anywhere in Australia. Thank you for supporting my small family run business.

0416 220 505
5927 Arthur Hwy Taranna 7180
www.eloiseemmett.com

Drinks

Nice non-alcoholic drinks are not just for kids parties. Many adults choose not to drink alcohol these days. Or there may be a pregnant guest, designated drivers, or just a choice to break up the alcohol consumption a bit. These drinks can be in a water cooler type drinking container for guests to help themselves to.

- Flavoured water with fresh fruits, try freezing them or adding frozen berries and mint.

- Fruity Green tea spritzer. Brew a iced green tea the day before add passion fruit pulp or mango puree and finely chopped fruits and top with soda water.

- Rhubarb shrub, combine rhubarb, ginger, mint, sugar and apple cider vinegar and leave at room temperature for 3 days. Strain and serve with soda.

- Elderflower or elderberry spritzer serve with lime, ice and soda.

Party Favours

Why not try making a thank you gift for your guests? A beautiful kiss biscuit wrapped nicely is lovely or try:

- Chai latte mix
- Choc or rum balls
- Kiss biscuits
- Jam
- Relish and chutney
- Bath salts
- Cordial
- Cup cakes

Party Games for Children

PASS THE PARCEL

Pass the parcel is a simple but fun game for children. The aim of the game is to be the last person to have the parcel. To get the parcel it needs to be in your hands when the music stops. The parcel has many different layers depending on how many people you have, but about 5 layers is good. To set up the game you need a prize, old newspapers, gift wrapping paper and sticky tape. Wrap the prize in gift wrapping paper (the prize can be anything that is trending at the moment like a barbie, face mask, anything small that the child would like as a gift that is small). Put the wrapped prize on the first sheet of newspaper and wrap it up like a present. You will then wrap up the next layers like this until about the fifth layer, which is the last one. To play the game; children sit in a circle and when the music starts the children start passing the parcel around. When the music stops the child who has the parcel unwraps one layer only. The children then proceed these steps until the last layer. Whoever unwraps the very last layer gets the prize!

SLEEPING LIONS

Sleeping lions is a very simple/ low maintenance party game that requires no materials and is still lots of fun! The aim of the game is to be the person laying still for the longest. First pick one person amongst the group to be the spotter. The spotter is responsible for catching the children when or if they move. If a child moves and get caught, they must stand up with the spotter and help the spotter catch people who move. In the game people can breathe and blink but that is all they can move.

BOBS AND STATUES

Bobs and statues is another low maintenance game that will get the children thinking. The aim of the game is to remember the order of the bobs and statues and how many there are. Chose a child to be the person who says how many bobs/ statues and in which order. Then the chosen one will say the order (e.g. bob bob statue bob statue statue.) Now someone plays the music, and everyone dances around, when the music stops the children must be whatever the order was for example a bob which is crouched down on the ground frozen and if you are last you are out so make sure to be quick. If the children get the order wrong or forget then they are out so they must sit down. And then we repeat these steps making sure to remember what comes next, to be a statue just stand up still frozen. Some tips for the game if the next one is bob then dance close to the ground so you can get in position fast.

DOUGHNUT EATING CONTEST

To play this game first make sure no one is allergic to doughnuts because the children will be eating them. The aim of the game is to eat the doughnut off the plate before anyone else without using your hands. To set up the game space out plates with doughnuts on them on a table like surface. Then get the children to stand in front of one of the plates. Say three two one and then let the children try and eat the doughnut without using their hands. Whoever finishes first wins.

MUSICAL CHAIRS

Musical chairs requires almost no materials except for chairs and music. Musical chairs is a fun active game for children. The aim of the game is to be the last one standing with a chair. To play start by counting how many people you have say you have 20 so start with 19 chairs in a circle facing outwards. Start the music and everyone runs in a clockwise circle around the chairs when the music stops sit on a chair if you are the only person not to get a chair then you are out. Now take one chair out. Repeat this cycle until you are down to your last two people (with one chair). Now it is hard when the music starts the two people have to run around the chair and whoever sits down first when the music stops wins!

MUSICAL STATUES

Musical statues is probably the simplest game in history. All you need is music and you are all set. The aim of the game is to be the last one standing. To play, someone will start the music and everyone will dance around showing off their best moves. When the music stops, freeze wherever you are as quick as you can. The last person standing still is out. Repeat this cycle until only one person is left, which means they win. You can also give out prizes to people you thought had good dance moves if you like. A tip for musical statues is don't do a handstand or cartwheel or anything you can't get out of quickly because it's hard to freeze!

TREASURE HUNT

Having a treasure hunt is one of the most fun games. The aim of the game is to find the most of whatever it is your hiding (chocolate, lollies, teddies etc). To set up a treasure hunt hide your prizes around in hard spots for the children to find, make sure they aren't looking where you are hiding them. Once you have finished let the children go crazy looking for the things you have hidden (most commonly lollies).

SELFIE HUNT

Selfie hunts are a newer game and are very fun. The aim of the game is to get a selfie with everything on the given list. To set up write a list with about 15 things on it. Some might be a fork, something orange, the birthday girl etc. Next give everyone the list and in partners they will find these things when you say go. Whoever completes the list first and shows you with evidence wins.

BLINDFOLDED MAKEUP CHALLENGE

The blindfolded makeup challenge is a very fun game. The aim of the game is to do your partner's makeup with a blind fold on. Whoever's make up is the best wins. Make sure to use your old makeup and don't ruin your good new makeup.

DANCING COMPETITION

This game is very fun. The aim of the game is to be the best dancer. Everyone stands around in a circle hyping each other up and two at a time people go inside the circle and show off your best moves. Whoever is the best out of your partners chosen by the circle goes back to the circle and waits for their turn while the other person sits out. You then must find a new partner.

THE TRAY GAME

This game is very reliant on memory. The aim of the game is to remember the most things on the tray than everyone else. To prepare the game someone must get a tray away from the children and put objects on it about 20 small objects and cover the tray with a tea towel so it is not visible what's inside. Whilst the children sit at the table with a pen and paper each. Next bring the tray out to the table and uncover it for 10 seconds the kids must try and store everything they remember into their brains. After the ten seconds is up someone will cover the tray back up and take it away. The kids get 30 seconds to write down everything they remember from the tray. After the 30 seconds is up the kids add up how many objects they have, whoever has the most wins. Make sure to check their lists that they haven't made up anything.

THE SENTENCE JUMBLE

This game is a good game for children that can read and write. The aim of the game is to make the most words out of a sentence that you can. To prepare, everyone has their own piece of paper and a pen. When it is time start writing as many words as you can (the words can't be names). An example of a sentence might be "happy birthday princess". Some words from this phrase are pirate, day, pad, thin, press etc. whoever has the most words after 40 seconds wins. Make sure to check that they are all real words.

Baby Shower Games

GUESS WHEN THE BABY'S DUE

This game is a lot of fun for a baby shower. Simply draw up a chart with boxes for your name and when you think the baby is due. Whoever is the closest to the date when the actual baby is born wins.

DON'T SAY BABY

This game is fun. When your guests arrive, you hand them a peg. If you say baby during the baby shower, then people can take your peg. Whoever has the biggest collection of pegs at the end of the baby shower wins the game.

WHAT'S THE STORY?

This is a funny and creative game for your baby shower. To play create a list of 10 things to do with babies for example nappy, nursery etc. Next make a list of 10 completely random things that have nothing to do with babies like jail, truck, book etc. in the story you have to include all of the words and you are able to use other words in your story. Whoever's story is funniest wins.

CELEBRITY BABY NAME GAMES

First print out photos of celebrities and then print out pictures of their babies. Put all of the picture's upside down in a pile. Now guests must match the babies to their moms within the time limit.

NURSERY RHYME CARDS

To play this game purchase a pack of index cards with a line from a nursery rhyme or make them yourself. Now the guests must identify the nursery rhyme from the line on the card. Once you have identified the line you can move on to the next card. Whoever completes the most cards in sixty seconds wins.

BABY PHOTO GAME

Ask each guest to supply their own baby photo before the event and print them out. Each guest then tries to match the guest with the photo, the person who gets the most right wins.

INDEX

B
BBQ Octopus with Baked Halloumi and Olives 118
Beef and Veggie Pie with a Cauliflower Top 96
Beef Wellington 82
Beetroot and Goats Cheese Salad 116
Bream Creek Pinot Double Cooked Beef 142
Bream Creek Riesling Jelly Strawberry Pudding 38

C
Caramel Macadamia Pie 108
Caramel Slice 42
Carpaccio, Tartare Red Meat 90
Cheese Ball Christmas Tree 144
Cheviche, Sashimi, Carpaccio, Tartare Fresh Fish 88
Chicken Noodle Salad 126
Chicken, Mushroom and Leek Lasagne 46
Christmas Fruit Cake 78
Christmas Pudding 74
Cob Loaf 44
Coconut Cream and Raspberry Clafoutis 136
Cray Cocktail 62
Crayfish Omelette 98

E
Eclairs 104

G
Green Peppercorn Wallaby Fillet, Roast Capsicum, Eggplant and Horseradish Cream 114
Grilled Rannoch Quail with Berries 40
Grilled Rannoch Quail with Walnut and Blue Cheese 100

H
Herb, Garlic and Fetta Bread Roll Christmas Tree 84
Homemade Fish Fingers (or Chicken Nuggets) 54
Honey and Soy Chicken Nori Rolls 64
Honey Soy Marinated Fish and Noodles 124
Hummus 150

J
Jelly 132

INDEX

K
Kahlua Custard 76

L
Lamb Mexican Meatballs 86
Lamb Sausage Roll 94
Lamingtons 70
Lemon and Port Arthur Lavender Tart 148

M
Miso Grilled Rannoch Quail 140

P
Paella 60
Parsley Dip 72
Pear and Apple Blackberry Pie 134
Petuna Salmon Glazed with Lemon Myrtle and Honey 102
Pizza and Scrolls 50
Plum and Campo De Flori Lavender Crème Brulee 130

Q
Quiche 106

R
Rannoch Quail Baked with Bacon and Tarragon 112
Rice Paper Rolls 48

S
Sandwich, Wrap and Open Sandwich Ideas 92
Skordallia 138
Slow Cooked Lamb 146
Smoked Salmon Pate 66
Spinach Pie 56

INDEX

T
Tassal Salmon One Tray Bake Rice Pilaf 128
Tassal Smoked Salmon and Corn Fritters 122
Toffee Apples 110
Tropico Co Prawn Saganaki 52
Turducken 80
Tzatziki Dip 68

V
Vanilla Cake and Butter Cream 58

W
Warm Garlicky Potato Salad 120

THANK YOU TO OUR GENEROUS SPONSORS

RANNOCH QUAIL

Rannoch Quail has been in continuous operation since 1979 producing premium Tasmanian quail. Originating from the South East of Tasmania, the quail farm started as a hobby and has grown to deliver a superior range of quality products. Winning acclaim from chefs across Australia, Rannoch Quail Tasmania aims to provide the best quality product available.

0484 002 519
admin@rannochquail.com.au
www.rannochquail.com.au

THANK YOU TO OUR GENEROUS SPONSORS

We supply whole, butterfly boned and hot smoked quail, as well as quail breast meat. We also have a new range of drumsticks, including smoked drumsticks available.

WHERE CAN YOU FIND RANNOCH QUAIL?

Customers can request Rannoch Quail from your local butcher or find at the following locations:

RETAIL STOCKISTS	WHOLESALES STOCKISTS
Wursthouse	Tasfresh
Vermys	PFD
Salamanca Fresh	Doppio
Hill Street (and others)	Freshline marketing (and others)

0484 002 519

admin@rannochquail.com.au

www.rannochquail.com.au

Celebrate - Catering ideas for perfectly imperfect home gatherings

THANK YOU TO OUR GENEROUS SPONSORS

EST. 1974

Bream Creek Vineyard

◦ TASMANIA ◦

BREAM CREEK VINEYARD

Bream Creek Vineyard is one of the pioneers of the modern Tasmanian wine industry. The vineyard was planted in 1974, making it amongst the earliest commercial vineyards established in Tasmania and was purchased in 1990 by Fred Peacock, one of Tasmania's leading viticulturists. We produce a wide range of award-winning wines, so we're confident we'll have a wine to suit your tastes. Beginning with traditional method sparkling wines, moving through a wide range of white wines and a Pinot Noir rosé, multiple Pinot Noir wines, a Cabernet Merlot and finishing with a delicious lighter styled late picked dessert wine. We are currently building a cellar door at the top of the vineyard with amazing views down to Marion Bay and Maria Island. The cellar door is due to open in April 2022 and we look forward to welcoming you for a tasting of our wines!

0419 363 714
fred@breamcreekvineyard.com.au
www.breamcreekvineyard.com.au

THANK YOU TO OUR GENEROUS SPONSORS

CAMPO DE FLORI

Discover a world of beauty at Campo de Flori. There's only one place in the world like Campo de Flori where a whole world of beautiful taste, views, and experiences can be had in the one place. We are the only farm in Tasmania offering farm tours of lavender, olives, and honey, with a cellar door for tasting and a ceramics studio where we can offer a true paddock to 'made here' plate on the farm.

Discover ceramics classes, have a farm tour to learn about lavender, bees, and taste the beauty of extra virgin olive oil and buy award winning culinary lavender, honey, and extra virgin olive oil from the farmgate shop. Located in beautiful Glen Huon, Campo de Flori is waiting for you.

03 6266 6370
lisa@campodeflori.com.au
www.campodeflori.com

PETUNA

Petuna started as a family company with a young couple – Peter and Una Rockliff – and one wooden fishing boat. Peter spent his time on the ocean, while Una sold the day's catch initially from the boat and later from a small shop in Devonport.

When they first set up the business, they shared the mutual vision that Tasmania could win worldwide recognition for the quality and environmental excellence of its seafood industry. Over the years, they have been central players in seeing that vision become reality.

In 2020, Petuna was sold to an existing business partner, Sealord Group who retain full ownership of their wild fisheries operation which began more than 70 years ago.

Petuna is committed to producing the highest quality, sustainably sourced seafood whilst responsibly maintaining the welfare of our fish and the environments in which we operate.

03 6421 9111
admin@petuna.com
www.petuna.com

THANK YOU TO OUR GENEROUS SPONSORS

TASSAL

Our Home is Tasmania, a beautiful island with cool waters and a rich maritime history where our ambition to produce healthy, fresh Atlantic salmon began more than 30 years ago. From humble beginnings, we are Australia's largest producer of Tasmanian grown Atlantic salmon, our focus on quality and sustainability has underpinned our reputation as a global pioneer and leader. The management of food quality is of critical importance and we have extensive policies and procedures in place aimed at the consistent production of high quality, safe food for all consumers.

1800 652 027

www.tassal.com.au

TASSAL SALMON SHOP

The Salmon Shop was created in 2007 as a centre to bring together everything that is Tassal salmon, giving us the opportunity to share our passion for salmon with the community. Located in a sea of galleries, theatres, cafés, craft shops and restaurants in Salamanca Square, the shop has quickly become a highly regarded fixture in this historic Hobart hub. More than just a shop, this must-experience destination includes a comprehensive range of delicious Tasmanian salmon products, deli stocked with delectable salmon accompaniments along with cook books and cooking utensils.

03 6244 9025

Tassal Salmon Shop, 2 Salamanca Square, Hobart Tasmania

www.shop.tassal.com.au

TROPIC CO

At Tropic Co, we are proud to provide high quality, world class tiger prawns with Australia's most sophisticated prawn farm network. Our farms are located across the coastline of Queensland and northern New South Wales with Australia's largest farm located near Gregory River.

Our farms, processing and supply chain is fully controlled and owned by Tassal Group, experts in aquaculture for over 35 years. We are excited to be delivering sustainable growth to the Australian Tiger prawn industry through innovation, technology and responsible farming, but our overarching strategy is to produce the BEST TIGER PRAWNS IN THE WORLD.

www.tropicco.com.au

THANK YOU TO OUR GENEROUS SPONSORS

TASMANIAN LAVENDER COMPANY

Tasmanian Lavender Company represents a total transformation of our family farm business struggling through drought conditions and trying to find a way to remain viable. We set about planting our first 10,000 lavender plants creating a new way forward for the farm's future. In 2012 we decided to take a leap of faith and open our business up to the public. We purchased a property on the waterfront at Long Bay and planted a further 6,500 lavender plants. In 2014 after two years of planning and renovating, Port Arthur Lavender opened its doors.

Port Arthur Lavender's quality range of lavender products are displayed and available for purchase in an interactive visitor centre and café. We now hand make around 70 different products showcasing our lavender.

Port Arthur Lavender Farm
03 6250 3058
info@portarthurlavender.com.au
6555 Port Arthur Highway, Port Arthur Tasmania

Richmond Shop
03 6134 8100
info@tasmanianlavendercompany.com.au
25b Bridge Street, Richmond, Tasmania

YOUR BUSINESS

See your business advertised here? For information about sponsorship and advertising in future print runs of this book and new books visit www.eloiseemmett.com

Little Norfolk Bay
EVENTS & CHALETS

Accommodation, Cooking Retreats, Workshops and Indulgence Weekends in Taranna on the gorgeous Tasman Peninsula. Perfect for corporate or private gatherings and celebrations. Contact Chef and Host Eloise Emmett to design your unique experience.

www.eloiseemmett.com
www.littlenorfolkbayeventsandchalets.com

About the Author

Eloise Emmett is a Trade Qualified Chef with nearly 30 years experience in commercial kitchens, including 7 years as the Chef and owner of her own popular restaurant The Mussel Boys on the Tasman Peninsula. She now hosts weekend cooking retreats and indulgence weekends at Little Norfolk Bay Events and Chalets a luxury accommodation retreat and boutique cooking school.

Eloise has been writing and photographing recipes for her popular website eloiseemmett.com since 2012. In 2013 Eloise co-authored the *Bream Creek Farmers Market Cookbook*, in 2015 she published *The Real Food for Kids Cookbook* and in 2016 she published the multi award winning *Seafood Everyday*. *Seafood Everyday* won **Best Fish and Seafood Book in Australia**, and **Best Book by a Woman Chef in Australia**. It then went on to become the third best seafood cookbook in the world, when it and won third place in **The Best Fish and Seafood** category at the **Gourmand World Cookbook Awards**. In 2017 Eloise published the first print of *The Tasmania Pantry* and in 2020 she published the second edition, *The Tasmania Pantry 2*. Both books won national Gourmand Cookbook awards. Her most recent book *Packed* was released earlier in 2022, where Eloise has shared her tips and tricks to preparing nutrient dense rich food on the go.

Eloise loves cooking, styling and photographing food and shopping for props at op-shops and markets. She has three children and with her fisherman husband and they live on the stunning Tasman Peninsula in Tasmania. Most of all Eloise loves educating families about how important cooking, preparing meals and eating real food. Her core message, is that cooking is not hard and is a lot more economical way to feed your family, and she encourages even the busiest families to prepare easy meals from real food.

www.eloiseemmett.com

Feeling inspired?
Would you like to learn more?

You might enjoy my Workshops or Weekend Cooking Retreats at Little Norfolk Bay Events and Chalets and a venue close to Hobart.

I teach:

Seafood Cooking

Bread Making

Photography

Party Planning

Self Publishing

Phone Photography and Food Styling

In 2023 I will be introducing classes for older children that include a take home meal for the family, classes for young children and shorter adult ed style classes that cover cooking basics for adults learning to cook. Keep an eye out on my website for all the details!

Please find more information at www.eloiseemmett.com

Eloise Emmett

CHEF   PHOTOGRAPHER   STYLIST

www.ingramcontent.com/pod-product-compliance
Lightning Source LLC
Chambersburg PA
CBHW042033030526
44107CB00094B/2992